DECODING YOUR DREAMS

DECODING
YOUR
DREAMS

Robert Langs, M.D.

Ballantine Books • New York

Library of Congress Catalog Card Number: 89–90938

ISBN: 0–345–36431–7

This edition published by arrangement with Henry Holt and
Company, New York.

Cover design by William Geller
Cover photo © 1986 by Chris Collins

Manufactured in the United States of America
First Ballantine Books Edition: February 1990
10 9 8 7 6 5 4 3 2 1

TO PHYLLIS,
DREAM AND REALITY

CONTENTS

viii   Contents

ACKNOWLEDGMENTS

The journey through the writing of any book is almost always a collaborative enterprise. I am especially grateful to Lenore Thomson for her contributions and her many constructive suggestions; to my editor, Channa Taub, for her help in reworking and honing the manuscript; and to Kate Josephson for her tireless efforts in typing its several drafts.

INTRODUCTION

When you first attempt to analyze your dreams, they seem to have as much in common with real life as the distorted reflections of a fun-house mirror. Don't be misled. Dreams are actually an extraordinarily reliable commentary on the life that you really live—the people you care about, the events you anticipate, the problems you are trying to solve. You will find that paying attention to your dreams is very much like having a personal counselor, whose entire reason for existence is to register your perceptions, work over your conflicts, and suggest potential avenues of response.

In point of fact, this counselor is a genius, consistently pointing out aspects of your situation and your feelings that you have overlooked or ignored or tried to keep at bay. What's more, the communications of your counselor are exquisitely wrought—rich in symbolism and imagery. It is this latter quality of dreams that renders them difficult to interpret at first.

This book is designed to teach you how to understand what a dream is saying about your life. Every dream reflects an essentially unconscious response to an emotionally charged situation in waking reality. As such, what you need is a method for translating that unconscious point of view into terms the conscious waking mind can understand and use. The method described here is *trigger decoding*, which will enable you to recognize the unconscious meanings of a dream as active responses to your daily life stresses.

Trigger decoding is a means of access to a view of ourselves and the world that is both strange and familiar at the same time. It permits us to make use of information being processed in the deep unconscious system, which is designed to deal with our hidden feelings and reactions as we experience them day in and day out. With this hidden intelligence in hand, gained by a proper understanding of our dreams, we are in a position to command an extremely valuable "second view" of the world. Properly understanding your dreams is much like grasping the underside of life—that stream of unconscious communication whose influence in the emotional sphere is so great that it outweighs the effects of the more familiar conscious stream. Dream knowledge is dream power. But this power lies in properly respecting its nature—and this lies, in turn, in the trigger decoding at the heart of this book.

PART ONE
CONSTRUCTING
A DREAM

1
DREAMS AND MYSTERIES

MYSTERIES intrigue us all. Attempting to solve a mystery promises an encounter with the unknown and the unexpected. A crime of passion executed with imagination and violence is emotionally compelling. The unexpected death, however grotesque, is spellbinding. So, too, are the pervasive sense of disquiet, the tantalizing clues left for the reader to unravel, the false leads, the moment of insight —the unsuspected culprit brought at last to justice.

Perhaps it will surprise you to learn that each and every one of us is a great mystery writer. Day in and night out we create our stories, filling them with passion and adventure and colorful characters—some perpetrators, some victims, some bystanders or witnesses. We leave ourselves puzzling, often disturbing clues that summon us to the role of detective. We even throw in a red herring or two to throw ourselves off the track. We challenge ourselves to search and discover again and again.

The mystery stories to which I refer are of course our *dreams*. Dreams are so vital to survival that almost all of us create them in clusters, four or five times every night. And it is through our dreams that we work over the emotional "crimes" perpetrated each and every day: the hurts to which we are subjected and to which we subject others; the anxieties and conflicts of everyday life—loss and accident and illness, success and joy and triumph, birth, death, love, and desire—anything that affects us emotionally.

Dreams contain clues that need to be deciphered. And some of these clues are very puzzling indeed. If we take their meaning at face value, we are likely to be deceived. We need a way to get at the meaning of these dream clues.

Paradoxically, although we are all superlative mystery writers, none of us are very good detectives. It is easy to be fooled by the alluring but often deceptive surface of the dream. We are ready to point a finger at an innocent bystander to avoid recognizing the actual perpetrator of the crime—not infrequently ourselves. This may make us feel better for the moment. But then we have to maintain our "ignorance" of the truth, and this effort usually proves in the long run to be self-defeating and damaging. And in the process we forgo the use of our inner creativity.

We are poor detectives for a number of reasons. The first is the nature of a dream itself. A dream is an expression of human adaptation to an emotionally charged situation; it is a means of coping with conflict and of achieving inner and outer peace. Since the correct interpretation of a dream leads inevitably to the real causes of our emotional disequilibrium, dream interpretation can provoke anxiety, even terror, as we bring to light the secrets that we have hidden from ourselves.

Too often, our fears triumph and our secrets remain hidden as we forget our dreams or ignore them or remember an occasional funny image to recount over breakfast. So there the dream sits, loaded with wisdom waiting to be decoded, with solutions to our personal mysteries and to problems we would do well to confront. Much of dream decoding lies in overcoming our natural fears and defenses.

A second reason for our difficulty in solving the mystery of our dreams lies in the structure of a dream: A dream is the end of the story, not the beginning. Recalling a dream is like suddenly finding yourself at the top of a mountain. You can see where you are, but you don't know how you got there. And you don't know why you came. You don't even recognize the context of your present position. To find out what's going on, you have to retrace your steps backward and downward to the point of origin.

Finding the origin of your dream makes interpretation possible; this strategy is essential to the *trigger decoding* method. Trigger decoding begins and ends with the point of origin of an emotional conflict. It enables you to discover the emotional conflicts and interpersonal problems that are disturbing your equilibrium and, more important, how best to solve these problems. Trigger decoding, then, not only exposes your emotional wounds, it also provides the balm for healing them—a form of healing that is not generated by our more usual conscious efforts at problem solving.

The third reason our dream mysteries are hard for us to solve is that they speak to us in an unfamiliar language. Dreams reflect premises and assumptions that are different from our everyday conscious understanding of ourselves, of others, of the world. Dreams have their own logic. For example, in conscious experience a sweater is something we own and wear; in dream experience, it is our total being, inseparable from our body and self. In waking life, were someone else to touch the sweater, that would be all he or she had done; in dream life, touching the sweater is touching you—your body.

The deep unconscious mental system, which dominates dream expressions, has its own way of processing information. This does not mean, however, that our waking view is real and our sleeping and dreaming view is unreal. Instead, each system—our conscious system and our deep unconscious system—has a distinctive way of processing and experiencing reality. Each has its own validity. The dream is primarily a product of the deep unconscious system. The problem is that conscious waking thought and experience do not allow the dream's realm of experience to enter its own accustomed domain. The conscious mind sees the dream world as a disturbing foreign body to be extruded rather than integrated. At the very least, we prefer to reduce dreams to the commonplace and to squeeze out their unique attributes to the point where they resemble ordinary waking thoughts. And yet, in preferring the familiar to the unfamiliar, the safe to the unsafe, we reduce originality to clichés—and lose much in the process.

Trigger decoding creates a bridge that extends from the deep unconscious system and its unfamiliar images and language to the conscious system and the everyday language with which we are quite at home. Trigger decoding is a way of outwitting our defensive selves, so to speak.

A fourth reason that we fail as dream detectives is the red-herring factor. Like all good mysteries, dreams not only embody clues, they also offer false leads that take us away from, rather than moving us closer to, their solution. Dominated as we are by our conscious needs, we are an easy mark for the alluring deception in manifest dream clues.

Dreams are loath to surrender their secrets. Of course, this is yet another way of saying that the dreamer is reluctant to know the decoded meaning of his or her dream.

A dream will seduce its captor into believing the answer lies here, when a far more meaningful and compelling answer lies there—in the very place where one has not thought—or dared—to look.

To put this differently, dreams are many-layered structures. It is all too easy to settle for superficial insights rather than peeling away the layers to arrive at deeper and usually more disturbing levels of self-knowledge. As a result, much of the thinking and writing on dreams seems clichéd. Clichés have a kernel of general truth, but they only seem to be specifically meaningful; at bottom, they are meaningless and empty. Their false leads distract the dreamer from arriving at more serious revelations.

Again, trigger decoding is a way of resolving this particular dilemma. Trigger decoding grounds the unmasking of disguised dream meanings in the flow of our daily lives; it always relates the dream to the emotional issues that most greatly concern you; thus, it grants access to the most compelling hidden meanings and insights contained in the depths of the dream. The deepest meanings revealed by trigger decoding are always surprising, but they are recognized immediately as inescapably accurate and pertinent to a current stressful situation. Thus, the solutions generated by trigger decoding a dream have great emotional impact, yet they often point you to self-evident answers to your emotional problems—answers that somehow elude you when you try to deal with these problems head-on through conscious deliberations.

In essence, we are great mystery writers and poor detectives essentially because of the way the mind is structured. We are faced almost every day with emotionally charged perceptions that are difficult to cope with directly. The human mind is designed to channel some of the most important aspects of these issues outside of direct awareness, leaving the conscious "self" free to contend with issues more amenable to immediate action.

Some perceptions that occur outside of direct awareness are not unconscious as such. Sometimes the conscious mind overlooks direct information or places it on some kind of mental back burner for later processing. Perhaps your eyeglasses need to be changed. Or your car sounds funny when you start it in the morning. A dream may bring such perceptions directly to your attention so that you can take action. You may find yourself dreaming that you can't find your glasses, or that the muffler has fallen out of your car with a clang. Such dreams are bringing essentially conscious information to direct awareness. The conscious system has its own unconscious subsystem, into which it may toss all manner of things it doesn't feel like dealing with. But such things are not highly charged. They are merely annoying or competing with other priorities for immediate attention. So they register only peripherally.

When perceptions and fantasies are highly charged and unbearable, the conscious mind doesn't register them at all. Such information is relegated mentally for processing in a deeply buried unconscious system to which the conscious mind has no access. When someone begins to perceive that a loved one is no longer returning that love, when an individual somewhere deep within experiences murderous wishes toward someone who has caused him or her pain, when forbidden incestuous stirrings press for expression, the feelings, perceptions, and wishes involved are so anxiety-provoking that most of the information is processed without any direct awareness of what has been felt or perceived or wished. If concerns such as these appear in a dream at all, they will be disguised and camouflaged. Lack of awareness is costly, but this is a merciful means of self-protection.

Dreams, then, are really like bridges that extend from the known to the unknown. To analyze a dream, to undo its disguise, is to give up a vital form of automatic psychological protection. The same motives and needs that lead to the encoding of dream material pressure the individual to avoid true decoding. At bottom, the dream is a mystery that only the dreamer can solve. And yet, in the solution lies knowledge that the dreamer may not wish to have. The dilemma can be excruciatingly painful. The outcome can be flight from the proper decoding of dreams—an all too common attitude, even among those who would claim to understand the unconscious realm. And yet, for those who have the need to know, who find the anxiety of not knowing greater than that of knowing, there is much to be gained. In the proper decoding of dreams, an intelligence, power, and beauty of mind is revealed. The very paradox that tethers life to death couples the incredible wisdom of the dream with fear and anxiety—and therefore with ignorance. We turn now to an approach to dreams designed to combat these very human tendencies, enabling us to tap the power of the dream and the vision of the dreamer.

2

WHAT'S IN A DREAM?

JODY IS A woman in her mid-forties. One morning recently she awakened with a dream whose configuration was both surprising and puzzling. As much as she could remember, it had been brief and pointed. In the dream,

> *Muriel {a woman some five years older than Jody who had long ago worked as Jody's assistant} is pale and seems to be ill. She comes to Jody in need of care.**

What can be done with a dream like this one? Does it really "mean" something? On the surface, the image had nothing to do with Jody's current life. And as far as Jody knew, Muriel was alive and well. For many dreamers, this is where dream interpretation stops. How odd, you might say to yourself, I wonder why I dreamed *that*?

But a dream is not an isolated story like a movie. No matter how obscure it seems, a dream is part of your re-

---

*All the dreams in this book are real dreams, suitably disguised to protect the dreamers—to whom I am grateful for allowing me to borrow from their unconscious creativity.

sponse to what is happening in waking reality. It reflects a situation that is causing you anxiety or conflict, but you are not yet consciously aware of those feelings.

Although a dream occurs while you are asleep, in what is called an altered state of consciousness, you are awake when you remember your dreams. This is why a dream seems different from what you normally understand as everyday reality. A dream bridges these two states of mind— two ways of experiencing reality—which don't speak the same language. Although you remember your dreams by using the language of conscious everyday thinking, the dream itself, as we have seen, shares qualities with deep unconscious thinking patterns. Therefore, to find out what a dream means, you have to stop looking at it as though it were a strange and illogical mixture of familiar and unfamiliar situations, and try to get a feel for the way in which a dream is actually conveying information.

If you begin with the idea that a dream is a response to a real situation occurring in everyday waking life, then the next step is to figure out how the images in the dream connect with that current everyday situation. For example, let us look more closely at the images in Jody's dream. The main character in her dream was a woman named Muriel. Who is Muriel to Jody in waking reality?

At the time she had this dream, Jody was the senior editor of a major women's magazine. Muriel had worked as Jody's assistant at another magazine fifteen years earlier. Jody hadn't thought of Muriel in many months. Why would she be at the center of a dream, at the heart of her dream images? And why would Jody dream about her being sick and needing help?

Although these images seemed at first to be very much at odds with Jody's conscious preoccupations, you can see that we are looking only at their surface appearance. A dream image is not a direct form of communication, like a statement. It is indirect. When feelings about a situation are not yet conscious, the situation cannot be represented directly in a dream. Instead, the dream will refer to another, different situation that has provoked feelings similar to the ones that are still unconscious. The feelings provoked by the substitute situation are already conscious or perhaps closer to awareness and not as disturbing as the feelings that are still unconscious. Often, when you recognize the comparison that the dream is making, you realize that the two situations are alike in ways that weren't apparent before. A dream, therefore, can often advise you how to solve a current waking situation or warn you against a certain plan of action.

There are a number of ways to find out how the images in a dream are analogous to a current situation in your waking life. One way is to think about what the images imply. Putting aside for the moment the question of just how the images relate to a current waking situation, your first step would be to think about what the images mean *by themselves*. Going back to Jody's dream, for example, we have the image of a woman who is ill and asking to be cared for.

Jody's first question, then, was whether she had some reason to be concerned about being ill. Perhaps the dream was trying to bring to her attention the fact that she needed to take better care of herself. There is some evidence that dreams do have access to happenings within our bodies unavailable to our conscious waking minds. Not a few writers have claimed that the first awareness of a personal illness is often found in the imagery of a dream.

But, as it happened, Jody could not connect the dream

image with an illness in her own life. Her health was fine, and she felt no incipient physical problems. On the other hand, Jody realized, her mother, a woman quite on in years, had been suffering from the complications of heart failure for about a month. At this point it dawned on her that Muriel is also her mother's name. She wondered whether the dream was simply expressing her need to care for her mother and to recognize her obligations in that situation.

Jody's attention to the implications of her dream images was clearly a helpful exercise, especially so because her dream was attempting to bring a peripherally conscious back burner issue to immediate and active consideration. On the other hand, although Jody's dream seemed at first to lend itself to a "back burner issue" interpretation, in the long run, this hypothesis raised more questions than it answered.

For example, if the dream had been attempting simply to reveal a peripherally conscious familial obligation, why would Jody's mother have been represented by a stand-in? And why Muriel? The mere coincidence of names seemed to be an unlikely reason for resurrecting Jody's memory of a former employee.

Jody needed to think more about this Muriel. Was there something special about her? What was it like to work with her? Was there anything remarkable about her? Did any particular memories or incidents come to mind? Perhaps the dream was drawing an analogy between the two Muriels for some reason not yet clear. Perhaps Muriel's illness in the dream was the dream's way of superficially linking Muriel to Jody's mother to point out some other more disturbing aspect of common ground. So Jody allowed her mind to wander freely in response to the presence of Muriel in her dream. She wondered if additional thoughts and images would connect this Muriel from the past to the events of her own current life.

This process of allowing the mind to wander without direction around certain images is called *free association*. Jody used it to find out what sorts of events or thoughts or feelings she associated with the different elements in the dream—not only with Muriel, but with illness, and with caring about someone else's survival and well-being.

To interpret a dream, then, you need to have both the dream itself and your associations to the dream. These associations help to create a waking context for the dream images. You might think of a dream as being like a compressed sponge. Associations to the dream are like the water that expands the sponge and reveals the many configurations otherwise obscured from view. By associating to your dream, you move closer to your current life situation as the dream has represented it and to whatever past situations seem to be relevant to that current situation.

Of course, a dream/associational network can be infinitely expansive, so you need to stay relatively close to current issues that may in some way be emotionally charged. Jody, in an attempt to target a current situation, considered that she had been recently contacted by a publishing executive, who offered her a compelling business opportunity. Eleanor had asked Jody to go in with her on the development of their own publishing firm, one that would specialize in fiction and nonfiction pertinent to women's issues. The risks would be enormous, but the potential rewards seemed even greater. Jody had been experiencing considerable anxiety and conflict over what to do, and the time for her decision was drawing near.

Although this seemed to be a likely source of unconscious conflict and anxiety, Jody was unable to connect the dream in any way to her current professional situation. But in thinking about it, she quite suddenly remembered that Muriel's mother had died during the time that Muriel was working for Jody. With some anxiety, Jody wondered if she was unconsciously wishing her mother dead.

So here is another "interpretation" to which this dream seemed to lend itself. Undoubtedly, as Freud proposed, dreams do reveal some of our darkest and most secret wishes, and associations to dreams can bring with them troublesome thoughts.

On the other hand, that a woman would have ambivalent feelings toward her mother—feelings of both love and animosity—built up over some forty years of life is hardly surprising. Muriel's presence in the dream was hardly explained by that sort of minor revelation.

Remember that dream images carry a number of levels of meaning. It is not "wrong" to say that Jody's dream was expressing her conflicting feelings about her mother's illness—both her desire to care for her mother and her wish to be free of that obligation—but it is a bit trite, if somewhat discomforting. One reason for the superficiality of this type of interpretation is that it is premature. We associate to a dream to extend the dream images, not to interpret the dream. Although associations may at times include a sudden insight, the dream's more compelling unconscious ramifications are not being tapped. It is, however, just this type of pseudoinsight that can lure us into settling for less—for a superficial insight that will permit us to avoid deeper, more painful insights.

In other words, Jody's associations did not reveal the meaning of the dream. They gave her a better idea of how to link the image of Muriel to a current situation in her waking life. Jody was led to recognize ambivalence in her attitude toward her mother's illness when she suddenly recalled that Muriel had lost her own mother during the time she was working for Jody. But Jody recognized this ambivalence not when she was free-associating to the image of Muriel, but when she was thinking about a different situation entirely—the publishing venture with Eleanor.

At first, Jody considered the fact that she might well be experiencing some ambivalence about the publishing venture. But the images were really more specific than that: They suggested that the ambivalence she was feeling involved the idea of caring for and ignoring someone's needs.

As Jody tried to relate this idea to the publishing venture, she remembered that Muriel had been very much involved in Jody's move to her present job at the magazine, which had also been a high-risk opportunity. She had been offered her present position when the magazine was still new, and it had taken her a while to evaluate the risks and make her decision.

Jody now realized that the image of Muriel actually connected the dream to both of the emotionally charged issues in her life—her mother's illness and Eleanor's proposal. Moreover, the memory of Muriel's role in the earlier job situation was an unpleasant and painful one. Jody had been offered the opportunity to head the features section of the new magazine, and the publisher had suggested that she bring two employees along with her as staff. So Jody had invited Muriel and another employee to come with her when she made her move. Together, the three women had created a very successful features section for the publication.

Within a year, however, citing budgetary problems, the publisher insisted that Jody fire both women. There was every reason to believe that this had been the publisher's strategy from the beginning—to exploit these employees by using their expertise and then letting them go. Muriel was enraged by Jody's acquiescence to the situation—that she would fire her two colleagues and remain with the firm herself. Muriel had lost control of herself and slapped Jody across the face. Jody had felt guilty and ashamed over the incident for a long time afterward. What's more, her reputation within her profession had been tainted, and Muriel had never spoken to her again.

Although this was still a painful memory, Jody had not actively thought about it for years. But now, the more Jody turned it over in her mind, the more it became clear that her dream was not so much about the decision to start a publishing company with Eleanor: She found herself squarely confronted by the conflict she had apparently been working over unconsciously. The situation that had triggered the dream was her decision to take two of her present employees with her when she and Eleanor started their company. Over the past three weeks, consciously, Jody had been debating the pros and cons. She had been confident that she could offer these two women a significant improvement in their job status. She wanted the help of these employees for good reason. They were especially well connected with women writers and would be an enormous asset in the start-up of her publishing firm. Thinking about it now, however, she saw clearly that the situation was strikingly similar to the one that had taken place at the magazine fifteen years earlier. Although she needed these employees to get the publishing venture started, if finances became tight, they might well become expendable. Jody had been concentrating on her own needs and ignoring the fact that she could not offer these women absolute job security. As a result, she was only dimly aware of reasons to hesitate in asking these two women to join her. Though she knew she was in conflict about the situation, the specific issues had been greatly blunted. Her own need for immediate support had made it difficult to identify and clearly acknowledge possible drawbacks.

We can see at this point that Jody's dream of Muriel was like a message from another voice deep within herself. Though not evident on its surface, the dream embodied a clear, however disguised, message to its dreamer: "Be wary of your wish to exploit these two women; the consequences may be the same as they were fifteen years ago."

With the disguised dream message decoded and understood, Jody saw clearly that she would have to go to the publishing firm by herself. She understood that some part of her did in fact want to exploit those two women, as she had unwittingly exploited Muriel years earlier. And Jody had the strength to face this manipulative side of herself, and to see to it that it did not rule the day. She decided to take the new job, but to do it on her own. Once these decisions were made, she felt an enormous sense of relief—despite a continued sense of worry and unease.

JODY'S DREAM speaks for an access to a distinctive way of thinking and coping—of processing emotionally charged information—and to a kind of intelligence, unavailable to us in our everyday waking lives and thoughts. Jody—and each one of us—is of two minds: one by day, and one by night. It would seem that these two minds think differently, and have different ways of expressing themselves, of having something rather different to say about the same situation. One speaks out directly and without disguise, whereas the other speaks only, or mainly, through disguises or en-coded messages—messages that need to be properly de-coded to be properly understood.

Dreams, then, have access to ways of experiencing the world and to resources that are unavailable to us in our waking lives. And clearly, dreams do not reveal these ca-pacities in outright fashion. By day, Jody's thoughts about her mother and about the job situation were quite direct. Her dream, however, dealt with neither of these situations directly. Instead, Jody dreamed of someone from her past who was able to represent both situations at the same time, and to suggest that Jody's ambivalence about other people's needs is a problem in both professional and personal con-texts. Whereas conscious thinking is direct, dream thinking is indirect. Although we acknowledge that some of what we feel is unconscious, we have not fully come to terms with the fact that the human mind has two very distinctive and often rather opposed ways of processing emotionally charged information.

Dreams, then, are as much a way of coping with our everyday emotional concerns as are our conscious attempts to sort things out and directly find a means of resolution. Dreams are not only an integral part of our mental beings, but are also wholly concerned with the issues of our lives. However, they speak from a deep unconscious system of the mind that operates entirely without our awareness, and whose contents reach awareness only through disguised or encoded images.

All unconscious information is not part of the deep unconscious system. As I suggested earlier, there are many situations that engage us only peripherally. We ignore all kinds of information without disguising it. This is because the conscious system has its own unconscious subdomain, which is a little bit like a catchall closet; it stores things we don't want to think about right now along with other kinds of nonpriority information. Information contained in this subdomain has been directly perceived consciously, but the conscious mind has tossed it into the To Think About Later bin. When we need this information, it is directly available to us, without disguise—though at times it can be difficult to retrieve.

In contrast, information that enters the deep unconscious system has bypassed the conscious mind altogether, along with its catchall subdomain. Such information is stressful and unpleasant or painful to think about consciously. So the deep unconscious system comes to terms with it outside of conscious awareness. When a dream brings an anxiety-provoking situation to our attention, it can do so only by analogy to other situations. So when we decode our dream images, we also gain access to the conclusions drawn by the deep unconscious system—the deeper self's strategy for action and solution. This is why dream interpretation is important: It taps the wisdom of the deep unconscious mind. Our conscious interaction with dreams quite literally helps to create who we are.

While thinking about the publishing offer, Jody remembered many things. She thought of others who had become independent publishers—their problems and their fates. She recalled prior experiences with Eleanor, and other risks she herself had taken in the past. She even thought briefly of her move to her present job—though not specifically about the role Muriel had played in that situation.

These and many other directly remembered, associated incidents occurred to Jody as she mulled over her dream and her predicament. With some effort, more unpleasant recollections emerged: Thinking about Muriel's image in the dream, she recalled a time when Muriel had been ill and there had been a dispute between her and Jody over sick leave. (Jody eventually felt ashamed of her attitude.) She also remembered a nasty incident involving herself, Muriel, and another female employee who accused Jody and Muriel of being lovers.

Memories that are not actively conscious but are part of the conscious system may be happy or sad, easy to remember or difficult and painful to retrieve. The point is that the unconscious "storage bin" which belongs to the conscious system maintains memories as they happened for a given person, and they are directly remembered and interpreted. As is true of all aspects of the conscious system, these memories and their recall are always straightforward, however personal in tone.

Not so with the deep unconscious system. All communications emanating from this system are transformed—encoded in some fashion. The conscious registration of this information happens indirectly and after the fact.

For example, Jody, with some effort, associated to the pallor of Muriel's face. Her thoughts gradually went to a time when her father lay dying in a hospital, pale and weak. She also remembered a time when she had seen a terrible automobile accident and glanced in her car mirror to behold an ashen, frightened face.

In Jody's conscious thoughts about her job situation, there had been no connection in her mind with extreme violence, damage, or death. Yet her dream/associational network reveals such images. (The associations to a dream image should always be seen as parts of the dream that evoked them.) The memories evoked by the image of Muriel's pallor were part of the conscious system, but the relationship of their implications to Jody's current situation was deeply unconscious. The world of experience that is tapped by our dreams tends to be far more elemental and visceral than our conscious waking experience. Here, for example, Jody's conscious view of a potentially harmful act (setting up two employees for possible dismissal) is unconsciously seen as an act of devastating physical destruction. Again, this aspect of the dream was revealed by Jody's associations to the images in it. If Jody had not explored the images for their emotional content, this deeper aspect of the dream would have remained unconscious.

This type of displaced and disguised representation is characteristic of dreams, but not of waking thought. Because of this, Jody's dream of Muriel opened up an entire new set of considerations about the present job situation. To cite just one of several encoded messages embodied in this dream—messages imparted from this deep unconscious system—Jody was indicating to herself that it would be unhealthy to take her two coworkers with her when she made her move. Thus, the image of Muriel stood not only for Jody's mother, but for Jody herself.

In addition, the image of Muriel represented the two women that Jody had been thinking of taking with her. The memory of Muriel's rage brought to mind a situation involving Diane, one of the two present coworkers. Diane had a violent temper. Once, when a girlfriend had teased her unmercifully about a former boyfriend, Diane had lost control and injured the woman. It struck Jody that under greater stress, Diane might even be capable of great violence. She realized that the dream was warning her in no uncertain terms about genuine physical danger to herself. If she took Diane with her to the publishing house, and it turned out she had to be let go, Diane could easily react the way Muriel did—but with a greater potential for violence. The most compelling encoded message of the dream, then, was that Jody's self-serving attitude was likely to invite more trouble than she could actually handle. The associations to the car accident and to Jody's dying father encoded this same meaning—using the raw and primitive language of the deep unconscious as a means of expression: If you follow your present course of action, things will get out of control and you may get killed. Repetition is a characteristic that the deep unconscious system shares with the conscious system.

That dreams speak with a voice different from that of our conscious thoughts helps to explain why understanding—that is, properly analyzing—your dreams is so important. Such efforts provide access to a world, a voice, and a set of resources totally unknown to your waking self. What's more, this deeply unconscious part of your mind is a major force in your emotional life—a force that you can know and reckon with only if you learn how to unravel your dreams properly.

JODY DID indeed decide to become a principal in the publishing venture. During this period, she also had many additional dreams which helped her to find her way through the difficult issues that came up. Two of them show how dreams can help us in surprising ways: Just three days before she told Eleanor of her decision, Jody dreamed that

> she received a letter from a reader of her present magazine. Both the letter itself and the envelope were defaced with gibberish.

Jody remembered having received two such letters two years earlier, when she had written an incisive but controversial article on women who become surrogate mothers. Quickly, through a simple use of decoding, Jody realized that she was telling herself something about her decision. The dream suggested that she was making an incisive move, but that the situation involved insanity in some way.

But why would the dream suggest any such thing? Consciously, Jody saw her decision as a difficult one, but it seemed eminently sane to accept a high-paying job as a publisher in a venture that had strong financial backing. But here, once again, her unconscious mind—her deep unconscious system—was telling her through her thinly disguised dream that there was something insane about what she was doing. The encoded picture was far more cause for alarm than the direct and conscious one. Indeed, these two views are often quite at odds. This is all the more reason to tap into the hidden meanings of dreams.

The dream led Jody to dig deeper into all of the issues and risks attendant to the move. In particular, she realized that Eleanor was a rather high-strung woman, much different from her present boss. Jody began to see that the new venture was really quite uncertain in many respects. In the past, Jody had experienced incidents of momentary mental disequilibrium, and she had struggled long and hard in her present job to gain a sense of stability and sanity. Jody's dream reflected, then, a deep concern with regressing in response to the uncertainty of the new situation to which she was about to commit herself. Although disquieting, knowledge of these anxieties alerted Jody to the necessity of dealing with these issues early on. Though somewhat shaken, she remained resolved to take the job, risks and all.

ON THE NIGHT before Jody told Eleanor of her affirmative decision, Jody had another dream.

> She is with a writer named Todd {a man who occasion-ally wrote for Jody's present magazine}. Both Jody and Todd are turning away from Frances {a woman who also wrote pieces for Jody's publication}.

Associating to this dream was both easy and reassuring for Jody. Todd had recently left his fifteen-year-marriage. His wife had supported him financially, but had also engaged him in a highly destructive, demeaning relationship. Todd had finally resolved to leave the marriage—to give up what was clearly a self-defeating, ungratifying relationship. Todd's financial situation was still rather shaky, so that the practical risks of leaving were considerable. But he was finally coming to terms with himself. He had called Jody just a few days earlier to let her know that he had taken a new job to ensure his financial independence.

Frances, on the other hand, was in a very poor marriage to a husband well known for his many extramarital affairs, but she had found excuse after excuse to stay with him, despite the fact that she was extremely unhappy.

Jody felt comforted by this last dream. Its disguised message was unmistakable: The decision to take the new job was a courageous move toward independence, and a chance to leave a secure, but self-defeating situation at the magazine. Indeed, it was only with this last dream that Jody had a clear and unexpected view of many of the ways in which she was unhappy in her present job. She realized that she felt trapped there with no chance of advancement but had been staying on because of her fine salary. She was in conflict with many of the policies of the senior editors of the magazine and distressed by the attitude of many of the other employees. All of this surfaced only as Jody decoded and came to understand the disguised meanings of this last dream experience.

How nice to know, Jody mused to herself, that dreams carry not only messages that reflect our most terrible wishes and our greatest fears, but also send us word that there is something strong and good about what we are doing—however unrecognized consciously. Jody was able to trust her dreams even more than she could her conscious thoughts, which were always so conflicted and uncertain—even when they seemed at first to be clear and firm.

There is something about the underlying intelligence of dreams, the indirect and disguised messages that they convey, that can be relied upon. We can trust them if we know how to discover their camouflaged meanings—*to decode them properly in light of their triggers*, that is, in light of the incidents that evoke dream responses in the first place. Dreams are not, however, easily deciphered; it often requires a good deal of effort and understanding to develop the capacity to decode them. Dreams embody a remarkable and unique realm of experience and intelligence, whose influence is great, and yet whose knowledge generally goes untapped. We can garner this mental power if we find the key to locating its treasures.

SUCH THEN, in barest outline, is the substance of how dreams are made and the value of accessing their camouflaged messages and meanings. Jody's dreams were understood—interpreted—in light of the life problems with which she was faced. Her dreams were treated as a reflection of an intelligence, a distinctive way of processing emotional information. This trigger decoding consistently uses the ramifications of trigger situations as beacon lights to illuminate the otherwise darkened and covert meanings of dreams.

Without knowing the triggers for her dream, much of Jody's efforts at dream analysis would have been guesswork. With a knowledge of the triggers in hand, Jody became engaged in a kind of guided discovery that enriched her view of herself and her life situation.

We will be mindful of trigger decoding each step along our way toward building a full sense of how dreams are formed and what undoing their disguises—again, ultimately, in light of their triggers—can tell us. We will find that triggers often elude conscious recognition, that they are often disguised in a dream instead of portrayed directly, and that especially powerful triggers are frequently concealed behind the more obvious and benign triggers we find relatively easy to identify.

We will watch, too, the interplay between triggers—external stimuli—and the inner mind that creates the dream. We will come to realize that trigger and dream are ultimately inseparable; without trigger decoding, a great portion of dream meaning and dream wisdom is lost to us.

So now, with trigger decoding perhaps a faint vision to be materialized later in the book, let's look at how the stuff of dreams is made.

3
THE MAKING OF
A DREAM

THE QUESTION of why we dream and how dreams are created has fascinated people through the centuries. And over the years, bits of understanding have emerged here and there. Freud, in *The Interpretation of Dreams*, synthesized the ideas of his predecessors and greatly increased our understanding of the structure of dreams, but there is still much we do not understand about them.

As Freud observed, dreams have a surface—what we call *manifest contents*—and depths—*latent contents*. That is, dreams combine both evident images (and at times, other sensory experiences) along with images or meanings that are not evident, but are embodied in the dream in disguise or in a way that is not immediately apparent.

In general, as Freud indicated, we get to the latent contents of a dream in two ways: by free associating and by interpreting. In the first instance, we simply let our minds wander about freely in response to one or another dream element. In the second, we bring to bear some type of unique understanding of the total dream experience that is not apparent on the surface of the dream.

All of this work is done with the dream itself. But a

dream doesn't just suddenly appear out of nowhere. We now go back to the beginning, to the moment of origin of a dream experience. Here, too, Freud can be of help. Dreams, he wrote, are instigated by *day residues*. And day residues are emotionally charged stimuli, triggers, if you will. Dreams are a response to trigger situations; they are part of our efforts to cope with stressful experiences. Before we look at the dream experience itself, we need to sort out the sequence that begins with a trigger. We react to a trigger in two ways. That is, we process the information (meanings) contained in the trigger situation in two different, parallel mental systems.

Our first reaction to a trigger situation is a conscious one. Something happens to upset us; we react directly, we feel a certain way, we remember certain things, we handle it in a particular fashion. In so doing we are activating what I have called the *conscious system* and its intelligence, memory storage capacity and the like. And once we have more or less settled the situation, we drop it and go on to other matters.

Simultaneously, a second system has been activated by the trigger: the *deep unconscious system*. Information and meaning conveyed by a trigger situation that is too unbearable for direct registration and awareness or has been perceived subliminally is not received by the conscious system. But such information does not evaporate or disappear. These meanings are received by the deep unconscious system, where they are fully and accurately *perceived* and worked over. The deep unconscious system has its own logic and premises, and some of them are difficult for the conscious mind to appreciate. In the main, however, one might call them *holistic premises*—for example, a part of something is understood as the totality; a possession is experienced as the possessor. Freud understood these ideas as primitive in character, but they are not primitive so much as indicative of the way in which we experience life in the emotional realm.

Up to this point there is no dream, only silent processing of a different order and type from conscious working over. But remember, the contents that are perceived and dealt with in the deep unconscious system can be painful and terrifying for the conscious mind to acknowledge. They cannot be experienced—reported on—consciously. The report, then, must be made in some other way; it must be transformed. Dreams are the transformed messages of our deep unconscious minds.

In this view—and there is much to support it—dreams are *not* a way of working over disturbing triggers; they are reports—encoded descriptions—of such mental activities. It is as if a spy has been at work gathering secret information. He then informs his superiors of his findings using a coded message. This coded message is equivalent to a dream. The message, along with the spy's own assessment of the situation, is equivalent to the dream/associational network. It is this network in all its fullness that we strive to decode in interpreting a dream. And clearly, if we know the trigger—the material being described and worked over in the transformed message—we are in the best possible position to decipher the disguised information we wish and need to know. Such is the substance of how dreams are constructed and then deconstructed.

The conscious system copes in very limited ways with highly emotional experiences; the deep unconscious system responds far more extensively, and knowingly, as well. Yet oddly enough—and this is perhaps the greatest flaw in the way the mind is constructed—this deep unconscious response, so filled with its own intelligence, is not accessible to us for direct adaptation. It is much like having a full report on something essential to one's development and well-being, but in encoded form, so that it is all but useless. (There may, however, be some benefit to remembering a dream, even if you don't decode it.) To use this information and advice, we need to undo the code correctly and read out the report directly. If we remember that the code was created in the first place to protect us from psychic pain, we can readily sense the inherent opposition in each of us to this seemingly simple and helpful process.

MICHAEL IS an insurance agent in his early forties. He and his wife, Louise, have two grown children. For the past year, preceding the dream to be discussed, there had been tension in their marriage—though not, as far as Michael was concerned, of serious proportions.

As a group health representative, Michael does much of the groundwork with clients in the realm of entertainment. On the day prior to his dream, he had lunch with a woman who was head of a sporting goods firm. She was planning to add a dental rider to the company's employee health plan and had contacted Michael's agency for a bid.

As far as Michael remembered, the lunch was the ordinary client/agent contact, but an odd thing happened when he was leaving the restaurant: Out of the corner of his eye, Michael had a quick impression of his wife seated with a man in a distant alcove of the restaurant. The impression barely registered: He felt a sudden involuntary sensation of panic, then realized that it was not Louise and shook the image off.

The lunch was followed by a series of appointments with potential clients and various plan administrators, so it was late when Michael finally returned to his office. His wife had phoned while he was out, leaving a message that she had been in town all day and didn't feel like making dinner, so why didn't Michael meet her at a restaurant. Michael was tired and didn't particularly want to eat out again, but he called back and agreed. After some bickering back and forth about where exactly to go, they settled on a place that Michael preferred. Michael then asked Louise what had kept her in town all day, and her response was so vague that Michael felt annoyed. He pressed the matter until Louise became angry. She said that she'd spent the afternoon with her friend Marge, who was thinking of leaving her husband and needed a sympathetic sounding board. Michael absorbed the information, then remembered that Marge was supposed to be away that week, visiting her children at college. "Isn't Marge up at Dartmouth this week?" he asked. Louise hesitated, then said something about her having returned earlier than expected.

At dinner that night, Michael realized that he was picking unnecessary quarrels with Louise, and wondered whether he was overtired. Louise, for her part, was aloof and distracted, and did little to ease the situation.

At home and preparing for bed, Louise suddenly became seductive, but her intensity seemed frenetic and demanding, and Michael felt put off. Then Louise, quite unexpectedly, engaged in a suggestive, but rather awkward dance, which both embarrassed and repelled Michael. Once in bed, they hardly spoke.

The following morning, Michael awakened and immediately remembered a dream.

He is sitting at an outdoor restaurant. He gets up and begins to cook his dinner on a grill. As he does so, he watches his wife ice-skating on a pond in front of the restaurant. He takes a hot dog off the grill and bites into it. His wife says, "Let's go to a different restaurant." Michael feels frustrated and confused, and angry as well. He turns away for just a second and when he turns back, his wife has disappeared, though the area is an open expanse and there is nowhere to hide.

Michael wondered whether the dream had actually awakened him; it wasn't nearly time to get up and get ready for work. So Michael took advantage of the time to associate to the dream. The outdoor restaurant, though different, reminded him of the restaurant he had been to the day before with the sporting goods client. During the summer, tables were set up on an outside veranda that overlooks a small lake. Because the veranda was set off from the restaurant and unobtrusive, it was not infrequently the site of trysts between illicit lovers. Michael had recently become aware of that.

The ice skating made Michael think, again, about his new client. He also connected the skating to the somewhat obscene and disquieting dance that had so repelled him the night before.

So far, nothing seemed particularly interesting to Michael. He went on to the next image, thinking that Freud would have understood the hot dog as a blatant phallic symbol. What would that mean anyhow? He didn't know. So he moved on to the image of his wife suggesting a different restaurant, which he was able to link immediately to the argument the night before about where to meet Louise for dinner.

Michael was beginning to suspect that the feelings in the dream somehow reflected his feelings toward Louise. He connected her disappearance/absence with her aloofness at dinner and in bed afterward.

At this point, Michael was ready to dismiss his dream and his associations to it as rather trivial, or obvious, if disconnected. But while he was moving to get up, Michael suddenly remembered a time when his parents were having marital problems. He remembered his own feeling of panic when his mother confronted his father with clear evidence of his infidelity. With a start, he recalled that she had sarcastically called her husband a "hot dog"—the sort of immature man who needs to call attention to himself by engaging in dangerous stunts. Michael saw that the words connected not only to the hot dog image in his dream, but also to his earlier associations to illicit lovers on the veranda.

And now Michael remembered his fleeting impression that he'd seen Louise with another man at the restaurant, and he felt that same sense of impending panic. Had it been Louise after all? Had she been lying to him about where she spent the afternoon?

A host of new images flooded his mind—his having pushed Louise to tell him where she'd been, the memory of a friend who had bullied his wife until she confessed her infidelity, the thought of a cabin near a pond where he had spent the day with a married woman when he himself was still single. He hated what he was thinking, but he realized that he had been ignoring all manner of small signs that suggested Louise was having an affair. Angrily, Michael had the quick image of confronting her violently, and recognized that the last scene of the dream was a literalization of the wish that he could be rid of her, or that all of this would just disappear so he didn't have to see it. Depressed and anxious, Michael got out of bed, steeped in conflict and concern, but also wiser. He wondered why he hadn't put the clues together before.

WE CAN NOW look at the making of a dream in greater detail. Dreams are encoded messages you send to yourself and, at times, intend for others as well. The messages you create in your mind are responses to incoming information, to prior messages from others and from yourself, embodied in moments, situations, and experiences. Once imparted, these messages evoke new responses from within and without. The process is continuous and circular.

As you can see quite clearly with Michael, dream messages are part of the flow of our daily lives. A dream reflects the operation of the mind as it attempts to assimilate or work over the incidents of the day, and to deal with them in some fashion.

When I say that dreams are a way station between yesterday's emotional issues and tomorrow's responses, I mean that dreams are more than a record of unconscious impressions. They reflect efforts to sort out the incoming information, to connect it to the past and future, to bring to bear a wisdom and intelligence, and to arrive at tentative decisions and conclusions.

In keeping with our heritage as physical organisms, our first concern is survival from day to day, moment to moment. We spend a portion of our time each day seeking out ways to ensure this survival, and we use other segments of time defending or protecting ourselves from dangerous situations that threaten that survival. And then, when time permits, we seek out a bit of pleasure or creativity—or simple rest. When all else is assured, such as when we are safe in bed, we also take some time to work over our emotional issues and to heal our psychological wounds.

In these efforts to cope and survive, we are, as I said, active in a variety of ways during the day. We respond to incoming threats, thoughts, and feelings, work out strategies of adaptation, and draw on all available resources. Some of these activities take place without ever reaching direct awareness—though they may be retrieved later on. Much of this effort is, however, quite conscious and straightforward. We define the realities involved, determine their meanings, figure out our options, take notice of their consequences, and behave accordingly. We turn to a storehouse of directly available memories that will inform us how one or another reaction has turned out in the past—indeed, our very perception of the situation will be colored by these memories. We therefore alternate between this type of direct retrieval of past memories, and a further evaluation of the current situation—we determine what to expect in the future and how to respond in the here and now. And although these processes are, indeed, under unconscious influence, they take place almost entirely in the realm of conscious awareness—we know quite well what the issues are and how we are reacting to them.

As a rule, conscious efforts at coping are consonant with consensually validated reality, and they make full use of common logic. We accept and work with reality on its own terms. An oncoming car is an oncoming car. We respond quickly and in keeping with past experiences and immediate anticipations. Symbolic thought and encoded images would clearly interfere with much-needed direct responses. For example, if a car is coming at you head-on, you don't stop to think about the car being part of the driver's self-image or a statement about his sexual prowess. You just get out of the way.

Similar rules apply to emotionally charged information and to how you consciously process such incoming messages. A threat of betrayal is just that—a threat of betrayal. And just as an oncoming car is a stimulus, so is an emotionally charged trigger. We have conscious and direct reactions to such triggers. But unlike our direct response to an oncoming car, our conscious reactions to emotional triggers are not confined to immediate thoughts and behaviors; they continue until we experience a point of resolution—or weariness. To a limited extent, these conscious reactions contribute to the formation of dreams. Thus, our perceptions of people and situations during the day often appear in the manifest dream itself. As such, though, they add little to our understanding.

For example, Michael dreamed of an outdoor restaurant similar to the one at which he had taken a client to lunch. And he dreamed of watching his wife engage in a somewhat exhibitionistic activity, which reminded him of her dance in the bedroom. Though the conscious perceptions are altered, they can be identified in the dream.

Along similar lines, the request for a different restaurant was "day residue"—it had literally been part of a direct discussion between Michael and Louise. And the feelings Michael experienced in the dream were part of his conscious reaction to Louise's behaviors. Finally, Louise's disappearance in the dream reflects Michael's conscious awareness of her absent mood during their dinner and in bed later that night.

In part, then, a dream reflects a continuing effort to work through our conscious reactions to emotionally charged triggers. Some of these responses are evident on the surface of the dream—in its manifest contents—but some are disguised in the dream. Overall, this connection between wakeful responses to a disturbing incident and aspects of dream imagery tell us that efforts at coping initiated during the day are continued at night and are reflected in dreams.

Melinda's father died recently, and she had a dream that he was alive. In this case, the connection between the trigger and the manifest dream is all too clear.

AFTER ALLAN's boss threatened to dismiss him, Allan dreamed that

> *his father was locking him out of their house.*

Here, the traumatic situation is not portrayed in the surface of the dream. But the main issue worrying Allan at the time of the dream—that he might be fired—is clearly conveyed in disguised form in the dream imagery. In reacting to charged triggers, we weave a complex fabric of conscious and unconscious reactions and themes, some manifest and direct, others latent and indirect or disguised.

You can see, too, that understanding how and why dreams are made must involve a search for triggers. Even the surface layer of a dream makes far more sense when you know what triggered it, and reaching the deeper levels is only possible through trigger decoding.

The manifest dream often reflects clues that take us back to the stimulus situation that set off the processing reflected in the dream. Though many people believe that if something is bothering us, it haunts our conscious minds, actually we often forget or repress or obliterate the memory of an emotionally disturbing experience. The more severe the trauma, the more likely it is that the conscious mind will put some or all of it aside—although this almost never happens in the deep unconscious system. To understand how and why dreams are created, it is essential to discover the day residues we are most likely to repress.

Think of it this way: Triggers rather than dreams are the crucial emotional issue. Later on we will not actually be interpreting dreams, we will be interpreting triggers. Dreams are simply a part of your conscious and unconscious reactions to these triggers. Still, the way to get to the meaningful surface and depths of these reactions is by associating to and working through dreams, rather than triggers. When you deal only with the trigger incidents themselves, you inevitably shift into a conscious mode of thought, which traps you and then confines you to direct and manifest reactions. Such responses are extremely limited and not fully adequate to the emotional challenge. On the other hand, associating to dreams opens access to the deep unconscious system, and gives you an opportunity to discover the breadth and depth of all that is stirred up by these difficult experiences.

Let us look more closely at the workings of the deep unconscious system. Because the conscious system is designed for immediate action, it often misperceives, fails to see, or slants our view away from the most painful attributes or implications of a disturbing experience. It is in the deep unconscious system that we process the most painful and terrifying aspects of emotionally charged triggers—dimensions that the conscious system is not equipped to handle, either because they are too disturbing or too complicated and unlikely to issue in a direct and logical form of response.

The human mind is constructed in such a way as to

spare itself or at least minimize immediate and direct psychic pain. Of course, we are generally aware of very painful situations such as a serious illness or blatant hurts by others; but the mind possesses a variety of automatic and protective responses that blunt or help us escape from the acute pain of such experiences.

In addition to direct and evident traumas, a hurt may be indirect or implied. Someone may defeat your expectations, call your self-worth into question, neglect to reassure you, compare you unfavorably to another. Experiences of this sort are generally not immediately apparent, but are intuited—read in a tone of voice, measured subliminally against a desired and anticipated reaction that didn't happen. In such instances, we automatically tend to shut off awareness to the clues we are picking up, but they are in fact being registered in the deep unconscious system. The deep unconscious system contains all manner of raw and painful images that have been excluded from direct awareness, but are being processed all the same.

In the situation with Michael, the clues that he had picked up about his wife's infidelity had received fleeting conscious awareness, but in the main, had registered entirely outside of consciousness. There was indeed a passing momentary sense that Louise was at the restaurant with another man, but Michael was able to dismiss this impression from his conscious thoughts; he did not consciously work through the question of its reality and its possible ramifications. That task was relegated to the unconscious realm—he discovered its existence only by working with his dream. The conscious system had to decode the pertinent references to the information being processed in the deep unconscious system.

Michael's dream, together with its associational network, suggested that unconsciously he realized that his wife was involved with another man; the clues had been there for months, culminating in the half-noticed possibility that she had inadvertently been with this man at the same restaurant where Michael had had lunch. But his conscious mind had ignored these clues or dismissed them. Michael subsequently confirmed that Louise was having an affair. But Michael first came to know this consciously because he had analyzed his dream/associational network.

Notice that the dream brings together many of the clues that Michael had been taking in unconsciously and working through without awareness. In fact, the dream underscores its point in a way that was especially painful for Michael, since it involved impulses of his own. A fresh set of associations to Louise's ice skating led Michael to recollections of a cousin who was an expert skater. In his teens, Michael had been strongly attracted to her sexually. The cousin's blond hair linked her to Michael's client. Thus, another emotional issue that helped to trigger Michael's dream and to forge its structure was Michael's own unconscious sexual attraction to the client he had taken to lunch. Consciously, Michael had entertained no inclinations to infidelity, although he had found his client attractive. This is precisely the sort of impulse or fantasy that will be barred from conscious awareness; the experience is not only disturbing, but it has no realistic potential for immediate conscious response. The dream indicates that Michael worked it over unconsciously, and that it became the nucleus of other images constellated by his impressions of his wife's infidelity.

Direct impressions and recollections play a relatively small role in the creation of a dream. Mostly, they generate immediate sensory impressions that can contribute to manifest dream images. These manifest images often serve both to cloak and to represent symbolically aspects of information being processed in the deep unconscious system. The information in this system cannot and does not reach consciousness directly. Thus, it must ride piggyback, so to speak, on conscious images selected because they lend themselves as representatives of deep unconscious impressions.

Michael's unconscious perception of his wife's infidelity did not come through directly—as a conscious belief or impression that she had been seeing another man. Instead, it came through in a dream image of a restaurant where illicit lovers often meet. The restaurant image is the surface vehicle for Michael's unconscious belief. The restaurant portrays this belief in encoded or disguised form. Michael's unconscious conclusion that his wife was being unfaithful to him was conveyed indirectly, through the image of a particular place.

We can turn all of this around and say that the workings of the deep unconscious system are safeguarded by protective mechanisms—and those mechanisms ensure that all information leaving its domain will be altered, disguised, or encoded. Terrifying information can be processed as long as we do not know we are doing it—and we will never know unless we decode the system's disguised outgoing reports. We will call this Guardian at the Exit Gate from the deep unconscious system the *transformation subsystem*. It is a system that transforms the raw images and information processed within into a new, manifest image that expresses this information in disguise. It is this disguised image that we call the manifest dream.

The key steps in this process can be summarized: trigger situation—deep unconscious processing—transformation of the information—manifest dream. Because this is the route the mind takes when creating a dream, the major, or perhaps sole, means of accessing the information contained in a dream—the unconscious meanings of a dream—is trigger decoding. Trigger decoding reverses the transformations that went into the making of the dream. Knowing the stimulus situation that originally set off the process serves as a guide to the meaning of the images involved. With that much done, the raw images and processing of the deep unconscious system stand revealed.

TIMOTHY awoke with a start. He had dreamed that

> *the house of his karate master was destroyed by a hurricane.*

On the day of the dream, Timothy had been to karate class. His friend Chad had told Timothy a story about how Abner, another student, had arrived early and found the karate master involved in a sexual encounter with still another student, Diane. Chad and Timothy exchanged a few jokes about the incident, speculating on the various sexual implications of the master's black belt status, and soon went about their exercises. Later, Timothy thought about this bit of news, primarily to nurse his jealousy—he had been attracted to Diane, but he couldn't compete with the sort of mentor/lover appeal of their teacher.

This was the substance of Timothy's conscious processing of the incident involving the karate instructor. He had school examinations and other concerns to distract him. In Timothy's deep unconscious system the situation was rather different.

Let's reconstruct the sequence, describing it as it actually unfolded. (Usually, we work backward from the dream to the trigger situation and the resultant unconscious processing. Here we will go forward from the trigger situation to the unconscious processing to the dream.) Timothy's unconscious sense was that his instructor had done something violent and horrendous. His view of the man as a pillar of strength and integrity had been shattered. None of these perceptions and reactions gained direct portrayal in his mind. At night, these impressions pressed forward, were altered (disguised, encoded) by the transformation subsystem, and emerged as Timothy's manifest dream.

The dream, of course, states none of Timothy's reactions directly. These are encoded in the manifest images; they constitute the latent content of his dream. Still, if we look at the trigger for the dream and sense its possible implications, we can decode this dream—undo its transformations—and arrive at Timothy's deep responses to the situation.

The "why" of Timothy's dream is the emotional disequilibrium created by the behavior of his karate instructor. The "how" of his dream involves unconscious perceptions of meanings in the instructor's behavior that did not register consciously. Next, there is a deep unconscious processing of these meanings in a system where a sexual engagement of this kind is seen in terms of utter devastation and profound loss. This experience and its trigger are then encoded by the transformation subsystem to produce Timothy's manifest dream. The sexual incident—the main trigger for the dream—is nowhere to be seen. Nor is Timothy's feeling of disillusionment in his mentor. These are now embodied in disguised fashion on the surface of Timothy's dream images.

The transformation subsystem, then, stands fast at the exit gate of the deep unconscious system. It is a protective mechanism, guaranteeing that with few and unusual exceptions, none of the raw and extremely painful images that are processed and dealt with in the deep unconscious system will emerge directly in the realm of conscious experience.

The transformation subsystem makes use mainly of two fundamental mechanisms, first described by Freud in *The Interpretation of Dreams*. They are disarmingly simple for being so powerful a means by which we safeguard our emotional integrity and our sanity. The two mechanisms are *displacement* and *disguise* (the use of *symbols*). Displacement means that an emotionally charged trigger is taken out of its original context and is worked over in some other context. This other context is similar to and shares links with the original situation, but is different enough or innocuous enough to provide distance from the immediate trauma. Through the use of displacement, traumatic issues involving one person will be worked over in a dream about someone else—someone who shares aspects in common with the person who disturbed you, but is less anxiety-provoking. If you are having a problem at work, you may well dream of a similar, but less threatening problem you have or once had at home. We don't tackle emotionally challenging issues head-on; the mind works best in this realm by indirection.

Let's look at a clear example of displacement. Pauline was told by her surgeon that she would need a hysterectomy. That night, she dreamed:

She is watching a fireman being lowered into a well to rescue a cat that has been trapped in its depths.

Through displacement, the surgeon is represented by the fireman, and the removal of Pauline's uterus is benignly portrayed as the rescue of a cat from a well. This benign image, however, contains disguised references to Pauline's deep unconscious view of the hysterectomy as a violent and brutal assault. In her conscious mind, although Pauline was concerned about the surgical procedure she was to undergo, she was also remembering an earlier operation that had gone well. But in her deep unconscious system, she connected the procedure to an abortion she had undergone when she was much younger, an experience that had frightened and horrified her. This is why her dream image involves the removal of a living organism from a well. Even the image of a fireman connotes devastation and flames out of control. Through the use of displacement—and disguise as well (the two often go hand in hand)—Pauline has reported out, from her deep unconscious system, an image that has been both transformed and transmuted, one that is far less terrible and terrifying than the raw unconscious images she was working through in her deep unconscious system.

From the vantage point of awareness, then, our most effective processing of traumatic triggers is carried out by dreaming of something else. We mull over incidents—either past or present—in arenas different from those in which they actually occurred. Some people believe otherwise; they say that the best way to deal with emotional problems is head-on and direct, and that any other way is merely defensive. But this is to misunderstand the structure of the human mind. The most effective means of coping with emotional issues is an indirect one. The deep unconscious system silently carries out its adaptive work, and, in time, it will emit displaced and disguised messages that both reveal and conceal these processes.

Undoing the displacement in your dream images does not defeat the work of the deep unconscious system; dreams are in fact making the results of this work available to you. Decoding your dreams gives you access to these results. Without decoding, the efforts of the deep unconscious system may provide relief, but by and large the great power of the unconscious system goes untapped and unused.

DISGUISE, or symbolism, is the other mechanism that safeguards the reports from the deep unconscious system. A particular person or event is represented by someone else or even by some other experience. This is not the same thing as displacement, which simply transfers an experience from one arena to another. But symbolism depends on displacement for a context in which to represent the person or incident in question.

For example, Michael *displaced* his wife's seductive dance from the bedroom to an ice-skating rink. By using this particular setting, he could *symbolize* the dance in the image of his wife ice-skating. The image that results when a symbol is constructed is different from the initial, or raw, image, but it is connected by some thread common to both. The choice of a symbol typically reflects the inner mental dynamics and state of the dreamer. Again, as opposed to simple displacement, a symbol will add to the representation by conveying significant aspects of the original image.

In unconsciously choosing the symbol of ice skating, Michael conveyed a number of feelings involving his wife: the coldness he sensed in her despite her attempts to engage him sexually, her exhibitionism, his fear that their marriage was on "thin ice." Michael's hot dog image disguised and symbolized his unconscious perceptions of his wife's infidelity. In this image, you can also see at work the mechanism that Freud called *condensation*: whereby a single manifest dream image carries two or more unconscious messages simultaneously. The symbol of the hot dog connects Michael's wife and Michael's father—and Michael himself—through the common link of infidelity to a spouse; and the act of biting into the hot dog symbolizes Michael's feeling of having being assaulted or damaged on the one hand, and his rageful wishes to assault and destroy his wife on the other.

In the same way, the disappearance of Michael's wife condenses his perception of having been abandoned by her and his wish to destroy her for her infidelity; it also suggests his wish that he were not seeing the problem—that it were invisible to him, although the dream makes clear that this strategy is no longer possible. He could no longer hide the information from himself.

By means of condensation, conflicting feelings can be conveyed in the same graphic image: To destroy someone by cannibalistically devouring her is also to incorporate her—to keep her as part of oneself, to prevent anyone else from having her. In fact, the image of cooking suggests Michael's feeling that he deserves some credit for his wife's desirability.

Similarly, the theme of infidelity is linked in Michael's mind not only with secret betrayal but also with immature exhibitionism—the idea of showing off, being seen. These two aspects of infidelity pull together his father's cavalier attitude toward his mother (by leaving evidence of his infidelity to be discovered), his wife's apparent wish to let him know that she is attractive to others, and his own pleasure in being seen with the attractive sporting goods client the day before. The whole idea of going to a restaurant in order to keep a liaison secret contains this same contradiction.

All of this is unpleasant, some of it even horrible stuff. It can be dealt with on its own terms mainly because the deep unconscious system is constructed with its Exit Guardian—the transformation subsystem with its tools of displacement, disguise, and condensation. In a sense, we are capable of becoming aware of the most terrible truths about ourselves and others only as long as we are guaranteed we will not be aware of what we are aware of. This is the very paradox that makes coping with emotionally charged messages and information a possibility.

Looking more closely at Michael's dream, you can see that the same messages are encoded in many different ways. The secret betrayal/immature exhibitionism theme comes up in the image of the restaurant frequented by illicit lovers, in Michael's associations to the hot dog image, and in the image of Louise ice-skating. The theme of infidelity emerges both in Michael's association of the outdoor restaurant with lovers' trysts and in Louise's suggestion (in the dream) that they go to a different restaurant. This highly disguised image displaces and symbolizes her decision to choose a man different from her husband—an unconscious perception encoded in the manifest dream.

Dreams tend to portray hurtful qualities many times over. And yet, unless you engage in a proper decoding process, these insistent messages will escape you. Decoding is a trade-off: We undo our natural defenses and modes of protection to gain access to a special kind of wisdom.

PAUL IS an attorney. He was made partner in a prestigious law firm, but his best friend and closest associate, Gregory, was not given this honor.

On the night after Paul was told the good news, he had this dream:

*He is going up in an elevator to an apartment on the top
floor of a high-rise apartment house. Then he is standing
on the balcony, terrified it will collapse. He hears a noise
and turns around to find a man wearing a gray hat,
sawing away the railing.*

Paul awoke in a panic. As he lay back, trying to calm
down, he began to associate to the images. The elevator
resembled the ones in Paul's office building, but, much to
Paul's surprise, it also resembled the elevators in the apartment house of his new girlfriend, Sonia. Sonia had been
living with another man and left him for Paul. Paul had
met this man once at a restaurant atop the World Trade
Center in New York; he had been wearing a gray hat. Paul
recalled that his father always wore a hat, and his brother,
who had been unsuccessful in business, favored caps. As
for sawing a railing, all Paul could think of was his friend
Archie, who had died in a car accident. He had been a
builder who was fond of doing carpentry work as a hobby.

With these few associations, we can reconstruct the
making of Paul's dream. Obviously, the major trigger was
Paul's promotion to partnership, an enormously gratifying
moment that, typically, was not without its sources of anxiety. Consciously, Paul was simply pleased for himself and
disappointed for Gregory. The complexities of Paul's reactions and perceptions were left to his deep unconscious
system. Paul had unconsciously perceived an envious rage
in Gregory, completely at odds with his surface congrat-
ulations and genuine happiness for Paul's accomplishment.
Unconscious, too, was Paul's own terror that he would fail
as a partner, along with fears of failure related to his long-
term rivalry with his brother, where success meant triumph
over and humiliation of his sibling—destructive images

indeed. Paul felt guilty, too, about being successful when his brother and Gregory had failed—and Archie had met with death.

All of these images are condensed into Paul's dream, and many more. Through displacement and disguise, these issues find portrayal in a manifest dream far removed from Paul's office, from Gregory and his brother, and from the friend who died. It is only with distance and camouflage of this kind, accomplished by these remarkable transformation mechanisms, that Paul could allow into awareness any representation at all of these underlying conflicts and perceptions.

Yet there was more than this. His mind was so occupied with the import of his promotion, that he had for the moment forgotten another kind of success. Just a day earlier Sonia had agreed to see Paul exclusively. This, too, was a triumph over another man. And here, too, Paul felt himself "at the top," terrified that he would fail or that Sonia's former boyfriend would somehow sabotage his position. Again, the deep unconscious system registers this fear in visceral terms—as a mortal danger, being without physical safeguards, falling to one's death. And this fear also had connections to Paul's childhood. Paul's mother had indulged and favored him, while she openly and blatantly despised her husband. This situation had made the relationship with his father difficult.

Paul's current triumph as a lover had mobilized in his deep unconscious system many old anxieties and a sense of guilt stemming from his role as his mother's favorite. Paul recalled none of this consciously, yet all of it was activated in his deep unconscious system and reflected in its transformed messages—the manifest dream. As noted earlier, the conscious system has its own unconscious component, which contains the memories you can recall directly. But the deep unconscious system retains memories that precede mature conscious understanding, and the implications and meanings of these early memories emerge only in disguised form in manifest dreams and in other types of narratives.

TRIGGERS filled with emotional meaning, for better or for worse, set off the sequences that culminate momentarily in a remembered dream. The deep unconscious system is always in motion, out of view, and a dream is like a window into its processes. You can look away from that window or pull down the shade. If you choose to look through it, you must first wipe away the fog on the surface of the glass—by undoing the mechanisms of condensation, displacement, and disguise. In these efforts, you will be guided by your knowledge of the triggers that helped to create the dream and whose deepest and most painful meanings the dream reveals in transformed fashion. And this is the challenge of every dream: Use it as your way into the deep unconscious system or forget it ever happened. And even though this choice is seldom consciously acknowledged, the state of your emotional equilibrium depends on your decision.

4
THE LOGIC AND LAYERS
OF A DREAM

ALTHOUGH our usual way of thinking is mainly a product of conscious system transactions, a dream combines inputs from both the conscious and deep unconscious systems— from both our conscious and unconscious ways of reacting to emotionally charged triggers. Because of this, the dream is a layered communication. In fact, a dream has three layers: the surface (or manifest) layer, the middle symbolic layer, and the deepest layer, which encompasses our rawest perceptions. The communications of our deep unconscious affect us in a variety of ways.

There is a great difference between deep unconscious *influence* and deep unconscious *expression*. Influence is ever-present; often it goes undetected and is blindly internalized by a conscious attitude. (The conscious system not infrequently does the bidding of its deep unconscious cohort without any awareness of the collusion.) But expression is intermittent; it requires a vehicle. Dreams are such a vehicle, and so are most images, stories, and narratives.

Every interaction is under some degree of deep unconscious influence. The more neutral the situation—a casual conversation, a job task, an effort to study something, and so forth—the less role it plays. But as we have seen, the more emotionally charged the interaction, the greater the extent to which our reactions are dominated by deep unconscious influence—skillfully orchestrated, most of the time, by conscious considerations.

Most personal conversations are shaped by deep unconscious effects. When stories are told and images mentioned, they are transformed messages being conveyed. The narrative contains some disguised—displaced and symbolized—meaning. We seldom bother to attend to this *encoded* level of human communication; in fact, awareness of this level of communication can be troublesome and awkward and is easy to dismiss as meaningless. But there is another kind of nonmanifest or latent content to a message that we tend to treat differently. Every human communication has a group of immediate *implied* meanings which can be extracted directly from the manifest contents. Some of these implications we pick up and register consciously; others we miss entirely. (These unattended, unconscious implications are then worked over in the deep unconscious system.) Still, it is the transformed meanings we most neglect.

To give a brief example of what I mean, imagine a situation in which a friend tells you to hurry up. This message is direct and clear in its main meaning. But this message also has *implications*. It may imply impatience, anger, distress, warmth, or irritation. We will notice some of these implications and miss others. But, by and large, there is nothing *encoded* or *disguised*—displaced and symbolized—in this message. Therefore, it is likely you will notice all but the most anxiety-provoking implications of its tone and content. And what you may find anxiety-provoking depends on your own experiences and conscious state of mind.

Now, let's look at a situation in which a message has encoded content. Imagine that a student teacher is telling her supervisor a story about a student in her night class who is being unfairly treated by the teacher, but has said nothing about it, believing that the teacher would not take responsibility for his behavior even if confronted with it. Encoded in this story—through displacement and symbolization—is this woman's unconscious feeling that her supervisor is not taking responsibility for his unfair treatment of her. Whatever the manifest and implied meanings—of inequity, withdrawal, and such—embodied in this story, there is also a specific transformed message. It is this level of encoded or transformed communication that is almost always neglected by message senders and receivers alike. (Indeed, paying too much attention to this level of meaning is often seen as behaving in a suspicious, paranoid way.)

Dreams are structured like this woman's story. Consider Patrick's brief and seemingly simple dream:

Patrick's boss Steven, recently retired, has returned to head up the firm once again.

On the surface, in the world of everyday logic, the dream was about Patrick's regret that Steven had retired. In fact, Patrick had a great deal of affection for Steven and had become rather depressed when Steven retired. The firm, which specializes in creating industrial chemical compounds, had been in existence for a hundred years. Its early retirement policy was designed to keep young minds, steeped in technological advances, at the helm. On the surface, then, Patrick's dream seems to be a classic example of wish fulfillment, perhaps the first principle of dream formation stated by Freud. (Simply put, Freud contended that dreams provide relief from anxiety and desire by mentally fulfilling hidden wishes.)

In other words, this is the sort of thing that Patrick could have said—and actually did say—while awake: I wish Steven hadn't retired; I wish he'd simply taken a long vacation and was coming back; I wish they'd reinstate him as head of the firm. In his dream, then, Patrick had simply visualized this wish/statement as having occurred. And although there is a difference between the two forms taken by this message—waking and dreaming—the meaning of the message is, in both instances, identical on the surface. Both versions of this message also contain comparable implications—that Patrick misses Steven, feels unhappy working without him, and so on.

But is there, as well, a hidden yet encoded or camouflaged deeper layer to this dream? And if so, does it reflect a way of thinking different from conscious/waking mentation?

To answer this question, we must find another trigger for the dream. Granted, the dream was a response to Steven's retirement, but what else could have set it off?

It is at this point that we move beyond the surface of the dream to its depths. We will do so only briefly here.

PATRICK HAD of late been experiencing intermittent chest pains. He had dismissed the pains as mild indigestion, and had done nothing about them. The night before his dream, Patrick had had a severe episode. Though his wife had pressed him to see a doctor, he had staunchly refused. This particular trigger doesn't seem immediately relevant; at least it makes no logical sense in terms of the dream. Patrick experiences chest pain and responds by dreaming that his recently retired boss had returned to his old position.

Patrick's free associations to this dream, however, took him elsewhere. He thought about his cousin Elgin, a man who had a widow's peak hairline, like his recently retired boss. Elgin had recently died of a sudden heart attack.

On the face of it, then, Patrick's dream had no self-evident connection to his waking situation. But beyond the surface, a hidden logic was present. Patrick's dream contains a disguised or encoded message that denies the danger of death by representing an impossible reincarnation—the return of a boss who is forbidden to return. And that boss bears a superficial resemblance to Patrick's cousin—who actually died of a heart attack. In that image, then, lies a camouflaged denial of Patrick's concerns about his mortality—and his recent chest pains. The underlying logic of a dream simply does not become apparent until you connect a trigger to the dream images and create an associational network.

This is because the logic belongs to the deep unconscious system. The deep unconscious system is invariably both logical and sensible, but it does view the world through a lens that is different from that of the conscious system. To our conscious mind, this lens seems to distort reality, but this is seldom so. It is simply that we have two lenses through which we see a three-dimensional world. The conscious mind doesn't recognize the participation of the unconscious lens, and when it tries to look through the same lens, it sees blurred images.

The deep unconscious system thinks inferentially. Part of a thing or a person is seen as the entire object or person. A piece of clothing someone owns is viewed as that person. An experience of seemingly minor proportion, as viewed by the conscious system, may have a devastating impact in the deep unconscious view. We saw this with Timothy's two reactions to his karate master's involvement with another student.

Freud identified many of the special ways the deep unconscious system operates, but his view of the unconscious domain was different in important ways from the one presented here. Freud never fully distinguished the conscious system from the deep unconscious system; he was more concerned with transitions from one system to the other than with a view of these systems as distinctive (though interacting) ways of processing emotional information. He never quite realized how dramatically different the views and coping measures of the two systems can be— he was more interested in what they shared.

There are several of Freud's characterizations of the deep unconscious system—and of the underlying structure of dreams—with which I, on the basis of the consistent use of trigger decoding, would take issue.

Freud saw the unconscious system as a realm of needs and wishes (instincts) seeking immediate satisfaction and discharge. He believed, too, that opposites—mainly in the form of contradictory wishes—can exist side by side in the unconscious mind. The unconscious mind can only wish, he said, and therefore contains no negations or contradictions. We can unconsciously love and hate, simultaneously, though consciously these emotions are contradictory.

When we view the deep unconscious system as having intelligence and coping capacities, we develop a different picture of the deep unconscious system. We discover that the unconscious system is not bent on immediate gratification but is capable of working through an emotional issue slowly, weighing all the factors involved; if anything, it is the conscious system that acts quickly. And we find, too, that the deep unconscious system has its own values and its own intolerances, in that certain behaviors are experienced as quite contradictory and unacceptable. It is simply that the two systems have different ideas of what cannot or should not exist. The conscious system—at least as constructed in a Western culture—doesn't recognize violations of what appear to be the physical realities of time and space. For example, one cannot be both Tom and Jerry at the same time; one cannot be in Chicago and San Francisco simultaneously; one cannot be both an ally and an enemy. In the deep unconscious system, however, Tom can stand for—represent—both himself and Jerry; San Francisco can represent both itself and Chicago; and a figure can represent both a friend and a foe. On the other hand, where the conscious system will not recognize simultaneity of identity, the unconscious system will not recognize the simultaneity of certain roles or relationships. For example, a relative who is also a lover is always experienced as a contradiction in terms (because of the incest barrier), even though the conscious mind may accept the idea and enter into such a relationship.

In sum, deep unconscious perception, experience, and wisdom create a worldview and attitude that are far different from the way we consciously experience ourselves, others, and our lives. Although dreams combine both views, they tend to reflect more strongly our deep unconscious sensibilities. As a result, you should be prepared to feel surprised and puzzled, yet receptive to the information you discern on experiencing a manifest dream, especially after decoding it.

Because in dreams people and objects stand both for themselves and others, a particular time and place can represent several locales and eras, and nothing is entirely what it seems to be, it is natural to feel confused and to shrug off all hope of understanding the deep unconscious domain. Yet spending time decoding one dream and then another, getting familiar with the language of this inner experience, gives us a sense of wonder and insight impossible when we restrict ourselves to conscious experience. Our conscious minds create the prose of human experience, but our deep unconscious minds convey its poetry.

THINK OF a dream as a layered, composite figure with a base of stimulus-related raw perceptions and images, a middle layer of symbols, and an upper surface close to direct awareness. Each dream layer is made up of a thin, clear plastic, and on each layer of plastic an image has been drawn. The pieces of plastic are superimposed one on the other, and when the layers are all in place, one looks down on what appears to be a single, final figure. This image is the manifest dream.

In this metaphor, the manifest dream has its own distinctive image. This image may be sensible or strange. Whatever its surface configuration, however, it is actually a composite figure. Each underlying layer has its own meaning. As a result, the manifest dream represents and disguises all of the nonevident or camouflaged meanings that lie somewhat deeper.

When you approach a dream, therefore, you should begin with its surface messages and meanings. For the moment, don't concern yourself with the underlying messages. Just take a look at the way everything has come together to form a surface communication that is unique in some ways and not surprising in others. Sometimes this strange composite is disarmingly straightforward; at other times—mainly when the underlying layers are especially forceful—the surface seems enigmatic.

Once you have come to terms with the manifest content of a dream, you might think of yourself as peeling away this layer and confronting a new composite. While the manifest dream is often imbued with the same concerns that occupy you in your everyday life, this next level below it is highly symbolic. By symbolic I mean that certain images by their very nature automatically convey a whole network of associations and feelings; these images are not dependent on context, but convey meaning in and of themselves. Some symbols are universal, because common usage makes them recognizable to everyone; other symbols are personal. An example of a universal symbol would be the image of a lion, which signifies strength and prowess. Many of Freud's ideas about dream images—for example, that an oven or a boat stands for the womb—are examples of this kind of universal symbolism. Examples of personal symbols might include a song that stands for a love relationship, or a candy store that represents a particular time in childhood.

Certain symbols in our dreams serve to disguise the memories and fantasies and daydreams that populate our latent dream contents. These, too, can be viewed independently of the context of the dream.

Although the manifest and symbolic levels of the dream are different in character, you will notice almost immediately that the two levels are linked by *themes* shared by both levels. You will find that thematic connectedness is the essential thread that connects each of the multiple levels of a dream.

To illustrate, using Patrick's dream, the manifest content concerned Steven's retirement and Patrick's wish that the event had not happened or could be rectified. The main themes were those of retirement, endings, finality—and their undoing. This information was straightforward and sensible.

But on the next level, by way of Patrick's associations, we saw that Steven's retirement was a symbol for an early and unexpected death. This particular retirement was enforced by the company before the usual retirement age. Thus, Steven's retirement and early death share the themes not only of finality and perhaps irreversibility, but of an ending that takes place before the usual time. In this way, it becomes clear that reversing Steven's retirement is a way to deny death. Steven's return undoes the regular order of things, undoes termination, and restores a past situation that no longer exists. For the moment, then, we have the manifest and symbolic levels of the dream, which tell us about the shared themes running through the various layers that structure it.

FOR PURPOSES of illustration, let us put Patrick's dream on hold for the time being, and explore the nature of dream symbols a little further. As I said, the symbolic level of a dream is not dependent on context for meaning. We'll examine the following dream without benefit of the dreamer's associations. James is a writer who dreams:

He is in a museum. There is a center courtyard. He descends the stairs to the courtyard and exits through an archway where a redheaded woman comes over and takes his hand. There is an outer courtyard and a high solid iron fence. James tries to leave, but the gate is locked. He

*begins to feel anxious, trapped. A street person, ragged
and disheveled, comes out of the museum, key in hand,
and unlocks the gate so James can leave.*

Without knowing more about James and his associations, we can say a great deal about the dream from a
symbolic perspective.

On the universal symbolic level, the museum, as a pub-
lic place of lasting records and memorabilia, can be said
to represent James's past life, and that of his parents and
ancestors. Going by traditional symbolic correspondence
between enclosures and the female body, the courtyard is
a female symbol—perhaps his mother's body—as is the
encircled outer court. The woman who takes his hand represents love, the disheveled man, destitution. The key is
universally understood as a means of gaining freedom from
entrapment.

As for personal symbols, I will tell you that the museum
is where James met Tina, his wife. The redheaded woman
is a friend of James's who has four children; she is a personal symbol of fertility. The street man, on the other hand,
symbolizes James's brother, who is out of work and struggling to make ends meet.

What now of the fantasies, memories, and wishes embodied in this second layer of James's dream? We will not
follow James here through a long period of free association
but deal only with the outcome of his work: the fact that
this dream represented James's wish for—and fear of having—a child. The wish is represented by the redheaded
woman and by the museum—James's mother had gone
into labor in a museum before she delivered his twin sis-
ters. The museum therefore also embodies an encoded
expression of the memory of their birth.

ONCE WE have looked at the symbolic layer of the dream, we enter a transitional layer, in which the symbols are understood in context. This layer moves toward the deepest perceptions and processes through which dreams are created. Again, context is created by triggers, in that triggers, or emotionally traumatic events, create the context or framework within which dream themes must eventually be understood. Let us now go back to Patrick's dream of his boss Steven's reinstatement. In light of the trigger of Steven's retirement, Patrick's dream has one meaning: the theme of retirement and undoing retirement. But matters are different in light of Patrick's chest pains. That particular trigger gives the theme of retirement a different meaning—as an allusion to death. Dreams are so structured that a surface theme may well have several different underlying meanings, depending on the various triggers to which the dream is a composite response. In other words, the manifest dream situation actually embodies various responses to different triggers; the images—the layers of plastic—are "read" somewhat differently, depending on which trigger situation is being considered.

Of course, some potentially relevant trigger situations are not necessarily part of a dream. You can't simply pick a context and stretch the images to fit it. When you find the triggers that "fit," you will generally experience a flash of recognition—what some dreamworkers call an "aha" reaction. The pieces fall together and the composite not only makes sense but contains more resonance than you can perhaps encompass. Each image becomes many-faceted and rich with meaning.

THE LAYERS that we have been discussing—the isolated symbolic layer and the symbol-in-context layer—may be thought of as the *middle layers of the dream*. They are sand-wiched between the dream's manifest layer and the deepest layer, which tends to be especially potent.

This final and perhaps most fundamental layer of the dream involves direct and raw perceptions that are not disguised per se, but which have been camouflaged by the layers above it. Indeed, it is these raw and uncompromising perceptions—evoked by emotionally charged triggers—that are responsible for the creation of the various superimposed layers that simultaneously disguise and give meaning to the dream. It is this layer of meaning that reflects most clearly the workings of the deep unconscious system.

In Patrick's case, his raw perception was clearly that his life was in danger. As we peel away the layers of the dream and undo the disguise of Steven's retirement, we arrive at this direct but unconsciously experienced anxiety. And here, too, it is thematic threads that unite the various levels of dream meaning.

As for memories, Patrick's associational network eventually brought him to his cousin's heart attack. He recalled that Elgin had experienced what seemed to be a mild heart attack, but refused to see a physician, insisting that there was nothing really wrong with him. He had actually died of a second attack that came soon after the first.

On this layer of the dream is a memory image that appears on the dream's surface as Steven's return to his company after retirement. Yet in the trigger/context of Patrick's chest pains, this image of Steven returning, as a denial of reality, takes an alarming form. The refusal of Patrick's cousin to recognize the seriousness of his situation shares a common theme with Patrick's attempts to deny the seriousness of his chest pains. Strangely enough, yet in keeping with unconscious logic, the image of Steven returning to his company after retirement portrays on this level Patrick's refusal to see a physician.

I HAVE USED the image of a plastic composite deliberately. A dream is not structured, say, like an onion or an artichoke, where each layer is the same as the one that follows. Each layer of a dream is unique. The top layer is usually the least disturbing, whereas the deepest layer lies close to matters that evoke anxiety and terror. As I have repeatedly suggested, this creates strong unconscious motives to settle for surface meanings, and to avoid the next bit of peeling away that evokes so much anxiety. Yet, it is the progressive peeling of layers that makes available opportunities for mastery and growth.

Take another look at Patrick's dream. Had he simply analyzed his dream as a wish that Steven would return to head up the firm, he would have gained no insight into the anxieties evoked by his chest pains. More important, he would have failed to connect his own symptoms to his cousin's death, thereby missing his own inner and most critical warning: Denying the seriousness of symptoms, avoiding doctors—these can prove fatal. Though Patrick's conscious thinking and conscious system were opting for avoidance and denial, notwithstanding the risks involved, his deep unconscious system was attempting to warn him that such a course could prove both foolhardy and fatal. All too often, the conscious system is concerned with immediate priorities and ignores provocations for action that may involve complicated and long-term decisions. Serious issues find open expression more easily in the deepest layers of a dream, which reflect the unique view of the deep unconscious system and its own constructive avenues of conflict resolution.

THE RICHNESS of a dream message lies within a dream's layers, but therein also lies a ready invitation to compromise and to become defensive. There is a tendency to settle for viewing the more superficial layers of a dream and to turn away from its deepest and most disturbing—though also most meaningful—layers, believing you have seen enough. As always, in the uniqueness and beauty of a dream lies the potential for undoing its promise.

5
DREAMS ARE DREAMED TO BE ANALYZED

WHY ANALYZE a dream in the first place? Does the effort give you enough reward to justify the time, work, and anxiety involved? If, as we have seen, the conscious system is not designed to process information being worked over by the deep unconscious system, perhaps the attempt to translate that information from one system to the other is unnecessary—or even harmful. In other words, is it dangerous to tap this unconscious system by attempting to remember and understand your dreams?

Studies have consistently shown that this is not the case. In fact, my own studies have indicated that the very process of remembering a dream promotes emotional stability. Remembering dreams seems to diminish the likelihood of acting blindly because of unrealized pressures from inner emotions and unconscious experience and needs. It also seems to diminish the likelihood of using physical or somatic channels—such as asthma, constipation, a sore throat, and the like—as a way of expressing aspects of our emotional conflicts. It seems, then, that if we allow dreams to speak for our inner working over of incoming emotional stimuli, there is a lesser need for other "spokesmen."

If remembering our dreams is in itself helpful in maintaining our emotional stability, why should we do more? There is reason to believe that dreams are actually dreamed—offered up—for a purpose. And that purpose, as I have said, is the use of our second intelligence—that of the deep unconscious system. Dreams are dreamed to be *interpreted*—to be fathomed, decoded, analyzed, and synthesized, to be understood in multiple ways.

Speaking practically, analyzing dreams is an extremely helpful way of maintaining your equilibrium and your emotional balance. It is in the nature of human emotions that disturbance can follow both the experience of intense hurt and the experience of intense satisfaction. In other words, highly charged emotional issues can be either painful or gratifying—illness, death, separation, loss, financial setbacks; or, on the other hand, marriage, graduation, a business advancement, falling in love, winning the lottery. Dream-derived insights give you a way of handling the inevitable daily pressures toward disequilibrium, so that you can maintain an optimal level of emotional balance.

In this way, you can take stock of and work through—and possibly resolve—specific everyday emotional issues. As we have seen, dream analysis can bring into focus emotional issues that the conscious system has unwittingly and defensively set to the periphery of waking life. There is a tendency in the conscious system, and in our daily, waking thinking, to minimize, avoid, or put aside any emotional issue that we can find the means to ignore. Dream analysis takes advantage of the deep unconscious system's tendency to take on such problems. As a result, analyzing a dream will frequently lead you to an emotional issue of surprisingly great importance—one that you had all but overlooked.

Once alerted, you are in a position to both analyze the dream for its perspective on your problem, and to begin to work over that problem in your waking life. Both insight and direct adaptation or coping are fostered in this way.

Dream analysis brings a dimension to your inner mental world that widens its scope, creative potential, and range of self-awareness. In the long run, though often with temporary setbacks, dream analysis will help to build a better and healthier self-image. Dream analysis can also strengthen your capacity to cope, along with your ways of managing your inner and outer lives.

Dream analysis also broadens a person's experience of the world. That is, dreams provide access to a way of experiencing ourselves and the world at large that is simply not available through almost any other means. (Daydreams and spontaneous stories and images, as they emerge intermittently from time to time in waking moments, are also a means of access into deep unconscious experience, but analysis of this kind of material is far more difficult than dream analysis.) Though it is seldom realized, life without dream analysis is shallow and restricted; it lacks a critical and broadly meaningful dimension. Dreams enrich our conscious point of view and widen our arena of experience.

Finally, dream analysis provides access to an inner creativity that may otherwise go unnoticed and untapped. Working with a dream is almost inherently imaginative and poetic. This is another reason our culture makes little room for dreamwork; we tend to value the pragmatic and the immediate. The rewards of dreamwork are of a different order; they are long-term and gradual. The results are not marketable; they don't provide escape or entertainment. Dream analysis is a way of refining the self; consistent dreamwork opens up avenues of innovation and imagination that are simply not possible through any other means.

Of course, many of the insights available to you through dream analysis are disturbing, but many are quite exhilarating and liberating. And even the realizations that cause you pain will, as a rule, prove helpful and adaptive in the long run.

For example, Priscilla, a woman in her mid-forties, dreamed that

she is throwing away some spoiled prunes.

Her first association was to some wrinkles she had begun to notice on her face. Next, there was her worry that her elderly aunt might be developing Alzheimer's disease. Further analysis led Priscilla to realize that she had been much concerned of late with her own body: She had been noticing that the lines around her mouth were becoming deeper and making her look more severe; the last few mornings she had had pains in her knees after jogging; she had finally gotten down to her optimum weight, but her body was beginning to accommodate the pull of gravity, and her shape was changing.

Priscilla had been pushing these various impressions aside, but now her dream brought her almost directly in touch with them. She saw that her recent sense of depression, which included some rather uncharacteristic self-castigations, must have something to do with her failing body image. With this insight, Priscilla was able to do a bit of internal rebuilding to shore up her self-image. She also began to investigate what she could do about her various physical body changes. Dream analysis was pivotal in these new efforts at adaptation. Six weeks later, Priscilla dreamed that she had been chosen to be Mrs. Universe. At times, analyzing our dreams can be the source of great and un-expected reassurance.

WHAT EXACTLY is dream analysis? It is probably best defined as the entire process that follows on remembering a dream and leads to its understanding. This would include associating to the dream and then examining in some way the entire dream/associational network. Dream analysis first takes the dream apart, enriches each component with associations, then integrates the resulting dream/associational network into a new whole—a fresh totality or synthesis imbued with meaning.

In analyzing a dream, you will typically shift from non-directed free associating to moments of direct exploration. It is important to realize, however, that analysis and synthesis occur in stages and are promoted to their fullest extent by intermittent use. You should allow for an extended dream recall and associational period before even attempting to understand and synthesize the meanings and implications of a dream/associational experience. The process tends to be circular: Associating to a dream fosters direct analyzing, which in turn evokes fresh associations that promote new lines of analysis.

Dream analysis is, then, far more than a simple intellectual exercise. The word "analysis" has an unfortunate cerebral connotation, in that dream interpretation is really the emotional experience of a dream—efforts at comprehension embedded in free-floating associations that are quite out of control and often rather unexpected. The greater the distance the analyzer has from a dream/associational network—and the greater the sense of cold intellectual contemplation—the less likely it is that a dream analysis will lead to genuine and truly unexpected, fresh, and meaningful insights. Dream analysis is not a stale process, but a living activity embedded within the dream experience itself. Strictly speaking, an interpretation of a dream should lead to an insight—to a bit of genuine emotional understanding that has not previously been realized in conscious awareness. In psychoanalysis, an interpretation is defined as a way of making conscious something that was unconscious. There are, however, many ways in which this can be accomplished. As I have already indicated, I believe that the most useful approach is one that utilizes trigger decoding—deciphering a dream in light of the events that prompted it.

JUST AS THE dream is layered with meaning, each level disguising and camouflaging the levels beneath it, dream interpretations and the insights that they entail are also layered. We gain some insights by simply examining the surface of a dream. Priscilla dreamed about getting rid of some prunes, and she knew almost immediately that she was concerned about aging. You may dream about someone you love, and realize that he or she is on your mind for one reason or another. As I will discuss shortly, the surface of a dream often quickly provides us with insights that have escaped our notice while awake.

Beyond these directly acquired insights, there are many critical levels of understanding that can be reached only by undoing some aspect of a dream's disguise. In associating to her dream, Priscilla quite unexpectedly thought of her job. At first, she couldn't figure out why this association had come up. So she thought about her job situation for a while. If someone were to ask me right this minute what was going on with my job, she thought, what would I tell them? She had just received a promotion—that was the first thing. She felt good about it; in fact, she had been weighing her recent bouts of self-doubt against this feeling of success. But two days prior to the dream, the head of her corporation had announced a reorganization. Priscilla's new section chief was someone with whom she knew she would have difficulty working. The reorganization was a new *wrinkle*, she mused—an unexpected glitch in what had otherwise been a near-perfect situation. So this was the common thread that connected her job worries with her new dream image—a figure of speech indicating new and unexpected problems!

With this fresh association in mind, Priscilla was able to derive a whole series of insights from her dream/associational network and its analysis. In particular, she discovered a great deal about the ways in which she was monitoring the change in her situation at work. For one thing, she was experiencing the change in a very personal way—as though it were something happening to her that would have inevitable effects on her self-image and capacity to function. She felt the change as a loss of physical integrity. These were feelings that she could not have recognized by studying the surface of her dream. This level of analysis required the use of trigger decoding—an analysis of the dream in light of the job issues that had set it off. Insights of this kind, which often involve rendering conscious very powerful, heretofore unconscious meanings, are usually more painful and difficult to achieve than insights derived from the surface of a dream. They also tend to be more meaningful, and more directly related to our efforts at coping with emotionally charged issues.

AT THIS POINT, a warning is probably in order. Although it is true that everything we realize in the process of associating to and analyzing a dream has some measure of cogency and relevance, it is also true that some insights are relatively insignificant, whereas others are of profound importance. Furthermore, it is quite possible to arrive at a false insight or erroneous understanding—simply put, to be quite mistaken about the meaning of a dream. It is therefore vital to try to safeguard against trivial realizations and false impressions.

As I have said repeatedly, analysis and interpretation of a dream take place in the face of necessary and natural defensive efforts at self-protection. If a particular insight were easily come by, we would be aware of it without disguising it in the contents of a dream experience. On the other hand, the extent to which the conscious mind admits emotionally pertinent information—anxiety-provoking impressions, meanings, perceptions, fantasies, and the like— is quite surprisingly limited. It is these very limitations, of course, that make dream analysis so valuable. Still, the anxieties that preclude direct awareness of disturbing realizations will also tend to lead us away from those levels of dream analysis that would bring such insights into awareness. It is therefore necessary, as has been noted, to make efforts to overcome these defenses when they interfere with remembering and associating to a dream, and to make similar efforts when they disturb the dream-analysis process.

IN PRINCIPLE, then, you need to be able to *confirm* or *validate* a particular interpretation or insight into the meanings of a dream. In general, it is a self-satisfying and pleasurable experience to arrive at a new insight when exploring and analyzing a dream. This basically healthy attitude has its own dangers, however. We tend to believe in what we create, and to stubbornly maintain our own interpretations of a dream—even in the face of information or data to the contrary. This need to create your own meaning can join forces with defensive needs to avoid a genuine but unrecognized meaning, resulting in extended attention to a superficial or erroneous interpretation that will lock you into a false understanding of a dream. There are a number of ways to safeguard against this outcome. I will describe them here, and flesh them out later as we delve into the details of the various levels of dream interpretation.

ALL MAJOR insights derived from a dream should be validated against one or more of the following criteria:

1. A solid piece of insight usually involves an element of the unexpected, of surprise. Although this is among the weakest signs of confirmation, a genuine insight should seem to appear out of the blue, or at the very least, be startling or unanticipated.

2. A dream insight should be relatively straightforward, and should make sense. Seldom is a true insight so complicated and convoluted that it cannot be grasped. Dream interpretations may be complex and many-faceted, but the main point is often so simple as to be elegant and beautiful. A valid dream interpretation is also reasonable. Remember that a dream is the production of your own mind; you may not always fathom consciously the breadth of the concerns worked over by the deep unconscious system, but a dream can only draw on what you know and what you feel for its images and messages.

3. A dream-derived insight should be genuinely new. Dreams are a means of access to what you don't yet know—the unprecedented. It is all too easy to rediscover what you already know, or to "discover" what you want to believe. If an insight seems familiar, note it, but continue to free-associate to the dream, to generate additional elements of the dream/ associational network, and to engage in subsequent efforts at dream analysis and interpretation.

4. A new insight gained through dream analysis should fit with other known facts, impressions, and insights. Although unprecedented, it should feel "right." At the same time, a fresh insight will provide your existing body of information with new slants and new meaning. In other words, the insight should fit with, but should also expand, what you already know.

5. A solid dream-insight should unexpectedly explain and help solve existing puzzles in your personal and emotional life. Almost always, there are issues and problems—odd things that we have been or are doing, emotional symptoms, and the like—that we do not fully or adequately understand in our day-to-day lives. Sometimes we try to get direct insights into these puzzles using our conscious capacities. But more typically we keep our questions on a back burner somewhere, hoping for eventual clarification. Very often, it is the analysis of a dream that provides the insights that solve the problem. Furthermore, since dreams are prompted by triggers that are typically connected to the unsolved issues, it is quite likely that a solid piece of dream analysis will lead directly to the solution of both immediate and long-standing difficulties. Of course, the resolution of a really difficult emotional problem or symptom may take days or weeks of dream analysis, but it is not uncommon to discover that a particular dream insight provides a special and immediate key to an unresolved emotional mystery.

6. A dream insight should itself elicit another as you continue to associate to and analyze your dream. That is, when you've made a particular interpretation, your subsequent

associations will usually involve further memories, fantasies, and other types of imagery that are new and unexpected. At times, a valid dream insight will elicit another piece of the dream, a piece that had been forgotten. Or some new image or fantasy will emerge and lend support to the insight. An especially strong form of validation is the emergence of new associations whose analysis generates further new insights that support the original interpretation.

For example, when Priscilla realized that her wrinkled-prune dream involved concerns about aging, a dozen thoughts and recent incidents popped into her head that supported this insight. In addition, her thoughts moved in two directions, both of which further supported this dream interpretation. One direction involved her aging aunt, the other touched on a number of seemingly minor physical discomforts that Priscilla had been experiencing, leading her to worry about getting old. It was at this point that Priscilla realized that the setting of the dream reminded her of a home for the aging that she had once visited. This unanticipated element lent strong support to Priscilla's original dream-derived insights. This element led her to more associations and further analysis of the dream, at which point Priscilla suddenly understood that her feelings of depression and of low self-esteem had been derived in part from an unpleasant sense that she was not aging gracefully.

Thus, Priscilla's dream-derived insight was validated, first, by her surprise that getting older was on her mind; second, by the "fit" of this insight into other facts and impressions; third, by its explanatory power regarding her current feelings of low self-esteem; and fourth, by its elicitation of new images and associations that were relevant and appropriate to the original interpretation. In the long run, Priscilla's dream analysis enabled her to cope better with her aunt and with her feelings about herself. Which brings us to the next point.

7. In time, dream insights should be translated into new ways of understanding yourself and others, and especially into new ways of coping. As dream insights accumulate, and integrate into new wholes, they can lead to a host of changes,

such as making you feel better about yourself, resolving symptoms or conflicts, improving your interpersonal relations, and allowing you to adapt to virtually any type of emotionally related situation. The transition from insight into constructive inner and outer change is the ultimate reward of dream analysis.

8. Finally, the validation of a dream insight should extend into the future. Often, one or more of the dreams of the following night will involve a dream/associational network that in some important way confirms and extends the hard-won understanding of the previous day. A special sign of validation involves the emergence in a subsequent dream of some type of constructive and positive image. Following a major piece of insight, it is not uncommon actually to dream manifestly of the resolution of a particular problem or symptom. Nightmarish and anxiety-provoking situations are transformed into experiences with a more hopeful and optimistic tone. Especially significant are images in a subsequent dream of people who are functioning well and behaving constructively. In contrast, false or incomplete insights tend to be followed by dreams with ominous overtones and destructive figures.

We have covered in some detail the why and how of dreams—why they are created and by what means. We are now ready to put this knowledge to use. We know where dreams hide their secrets, and we know, too, how to unmask their hidden meanings. The time has come to solve the basic problem of how best to interpret our dreams.

PART TWO
DECODING A DREAM

6
CAPTURING THE DREAM

CATCH A leprechaun by light of day, and his pot of gold is yours. Catch a dream, hold on to it as it squirms and tries to slip through your mental fingers, and its valuable treasures may be yours as well. But getting to these treasures is sometimes more difficult than catching a leprechaun. But we are now well armed to give it a try.

John is a young man—unmarried—who teaches English at a university. One morning he awakened and had a strong sense of having had a dream, but its content seemed just out of reach. Unformed, unseen, its clouded presence taunted him. He could almost feel the dream, floating somewhere inside his head, somewhere in his mind. How strange, he thought, to know that something is there and not be able to fetch it out. Somewhere he recalled reading that much of what is in our mind exists as inchoate potential.

John lay in bed, tense and frowning, trying to get hold of the dream. An image of a car appeared in his mind; yes, the dream was about a car. Feeling relieved, John began to see more. The setting was rural, there were trees and a lawn. What else? John closed his eyes tightly and tried to bring back more, but nothing came forth.

Now John decided to relax a bit and let the dream come back on its own. He fell back into his pillow and allowed his mind to wander about. It felt a little like watching for the dream out of the corner of some mental eye. Some of the thoughts that returned to him gave him a peculiar sensation that the dream was close at hand. After a while, his thoughts came back directly to his dream. It occurred to him now that there were several people in the car. His dream seemed to be surfacing, but he couldn't remember enough to make sense of it. Nothing more came back to him, so John decided to drop it and go about the business of his day.

While eating lunch alone in his office at the university, John found his thoughts wandering back to the dream. He could picture the people in the car more clearly now. They were actors and actresses, laughing and having a good time. They wanted John to join them in their celebration. John remembered considering their offer, but what he actually decided to do was still vague. John's feeling is that he walked away from the celebrants.

As he was turning this dream scenario over in his mind, he was suddenly aware of a second dream. This dream was also difficult to bring back. As best as John could make out, it was something about a tavern, about people at tables. But the images were so vague that John was not even sure they had anything to do with his dream.

Most mornings, John was able to remember a dream or two. Sometimes, he simply dismissed them as so much flotsam. At other times, for reasons unknown to himself, John became interested in a particular dream. He tried his hand at surface meanings. He had read something about free-associating to dreams, so he sometimes let his mind wander here and there, without direction or purpose. And then he tried to make sense of what emerged.

In this situation, John was puzzled by his uncharacteristic inability to capture his dreams. And his usual strategy for dealing with his images wasn't helping him very much. He couldn't make out anything from the surface images of the first dream. John was dating several women, but none of them were actresses, though he was hardly averse to meeting one.

What more was there to think about this dream? John tried free-associating to the dream images. One by one, he thought of a dream element and allowed his mind free rein to go where it wished in response. His thoughts took him to a novel he had written and submitted to an agent. Perhaps the dream was reflecting his fantasies of writing a best-seller and turning it into a movie screenplay. But, then, why did he walk away from the car? Was John secretly hoping for the failure of these fantasies? Although most unpleasant to contemplate, John was now alerted to this possibility. His dream—more accurately, he himself, by associating to his dream—had suggested some possible self-defeating needs John wanted to search for, discover, and resolve. With that insight, John had his first reward for capturing his dream.

John found that he had two more associations to the dream. (Dream associations can be actively generated in response to particular dream images or they can appear spontaneously, "on their own" as your mind wanders about in reaction to a dream.) John's first new association was to the movie *The Godfather*, which John had seen for the first time two nights earlier. The second was to a conversation that John had had with his father on the night prior to the dream. His father had recently been suffering with fevers of unknown origin—with a vague and unseen, as yet undiagnosed illness. On the night before the dream, John had discussed this illness with his father, who was feeling quite depressed and convinced that he was going to die. John had promised to arrange a consultation for his father with a prominent internist who is well known for his diagnostic skills.

At this point, John suddenly realized that he had forgotten to make the appointment. Now the car in the dream reminded John of the black Cadillacs that carry mourning family members to burial sites.

With these rather shocking associations, John began to realize that he had very neatly disguised the scenario of his father's funeral in the dream. Had John any doubts about this realization, long-forgotten memories of his father as an amateur actor left no doubt as to the connection between his father and the dream.

Now John suddenly remembered scenes from his early childhood, when his father, in fits of temper, not infrequently beat him with a strap. These particular memories were strange and unreal to John; he had not recalled them in many years. They embodied John's half-fantasy/half-real image of his father as cruel and powerful and violent; the memories had been given shape by the themes of *The Godfather*, and John realized now that the black car also connected the dream with an image of his father as if he were a member of the Mafia.

All of this led John along two divergent paths. Along one, he had loving feelings toward his father. Those feelings were very much connected in his mind with the memory of a summer month in his childhood when his mother had visited family in Europe and John had spent the time alone with his father on a farm. John and his father had been close that summer, had fun together, shared long walks and peace. Were his father to die, John's loss in light of these loving moments and feelings would be great. Even the recognition of disguised but genuine affection for his father was anxiety-provoking for John.

The other path—one not uncommonly disguised in dreams—was overgrown with anger. There John felt his old hatred for the father who beat him. John experienced, too, an unbounded rage, along with wishes that his father were dead, wishes secretly gratified in his dream.

DREAMS LEAD us along painful pathways that are deeply camouflaged to ease our sense of dread. Yet clearing away the path, seeing the dream for what it is and what it contains, can be enormously helpful in the end. What we need is faith in ourselves as dreamers and as the only ones who can, after all, decode the dream and arrive at its brilliant, but more often than not, disturbing insights.

In John's situation, his dream encoded a deep ambivalence toward his father. By recognizing his anger, John not only understood why he had forgotten to make the doctor's appointment for his father, but he was also able to make sense of a series of recent provocative incidents with him. John had blamed his father for these incidents. But he could see now that his own unrealized anger had played a role. Beyond that, several nasty incidents between John and his boss—an older man like John's father—could now be understood as battles displaced from their point of origin, the tensions between John and his father.

Unconscious influences range far and wide. Their effects often go unrecognized—and uncontrolled. Capturing your dreams is a way of embarking on one of the few routes available to you into that mental realm that operates beyond direct awareness.

Moreover, dreams often point to otherwise unrecognized solutions to our emotional and interpersonal conflicts. In John's situation, this aspect of his dream involved a rather different trigger—one unrelated to his father.

John's attention turned now to a woman named Alicia, whom he was presently dating. The relationship was tense, John thought, chiefly because Alicia was also involved with another man—someone John knew. John realized he was unhappy with the situation, but he could not find a way of resolving it. He wanted to stop seeing Alicia, yet he could not bring himself to break off the relationship. He thought about giving her an ultimatum: Give up the other man, make a commitment, and he would commit himself to her as well. But this, too, he was unable to do.

John saw that his dream was in part a response to having had dinner with Alicia recently. Alicia was an attractive woman; John's friends said she looked like Sophia Loren. John suddenly recalled the actresses in his dream. And that Alicia owned a black Toyota.

In this light, John's dream—his unconscious mind—was telling him in a disguised way to give up his relationship with Alicia—to walk away from her. This bit of understanding led John to reconsider their relationship—particularly since this element of the dream also incorporated references to ambivalence and cruelty and death. Something in him was already taking steps to end things with Alicia. Ultimately, he did break off the relationship, and he felt much relieved. It was his dream that first made him aware of what he needed to do, and in a way that eventually made good sense.

It is more natural to forget a dream than to remember it. Dream researchers have shown that almost everyone has three to five episodes of dreaming each night. And if dream research subjects are awakened immediately after physical indications of dreaming, such as rapid back-and-forth eye movement (which occurs during so-called REM sleep), they will typically recall one or more rather lengthy dream experiences. To these we may add dreams that occur during non-REM sleep. When total dream production in a dream laboratory is compared with the average amount of dream material remembered by even a frequent dreamer, it is immediately evident that under the best of circumstances we are able to capture each morning only a small percentage of our dream output from the previous night.

Why are dreams so elusive? John knew that he had been dreaming, and he felt frustrated when all he could produce were a few fragments of what he knew to be a much more elaborate dream experience. He was able to associate to his first dream and give it more substance, but he was blocked on adding elements to his second dream—the one about the tavern. Clearly, although he was consciously determined to remember his dream, another part of John—another part of his mind expressing a rather different need—was determined to block access to the dream. Unknowingly, John was engaged in a struggle between a conscious wish to remember and an unconscious wish to forget. This struggle exists in all of us, even when we do not experience it directly.

The struggle against dream recall takes many forms. Some people remember few or no dreams at all, no matter how hard they try. Others remember anything from an occasional dream to several each night. But no matter how many dreams we remember, the massive number of dreams that each of us forgets speaks to powerful mental forces opposed to such recall. These forces are also expressed in the ease with which we often forget all or part of a dream—especially when we have recalled the dream in the middle of the night or when something more pressing in waking reality commands our attention.

Psychoanalysts call such forces "resistances," suggesting the expression of powerful inner needs, most of them unconscious or outside of awareness, of essentially the need to deny or not to know. Some psychiatrists even believe that dreams are a kind of mental housekeeping and are designed to be forgotten. This theory holds that dreams incorporate old strategies for action that are being discarded to make room for new and better ones. But this theory is not widely supported. The idea that a system of the mind would expend effort to report useless information has no comparable analogy in all of nature. There seems to be a measure of incompatibility between the way we think by night and the way we think by day.

Dream recall is favored by a variety of contrasting factors. An anxious dream or nightmare is likely to be remembered, as is a dream with a strong underlying message, but so, too, are relatively innocuous dreams whose recollection will not lead us toward extraordinary anxiety. Remembering a dream during the transition from sleep to awakening—while in both worlds, so to speak—enhances dream recall. And in general, we are more likely to remember a dream during and after an acutely stressful experience (trigger)—it is then that we most need to use our deep unconscious intelligence.

The reasons for this conflict between remembering and forgetting dreams have already received ample attention. We have seen several instances of the conflict between wanting to obliterate a dream experience (because the dream and its underlying issues are too painful to deal with consciously, even with the use of disguise) and needing to recall—and eventually decode—a dream (because we need to master an emotional conflict).

To elaborate on previous discussions: For unclear psychobiological reasons, the human mind has evolved two separate but interacting systems for dealing with the vicissitudes of life and existence. The first, the *conscious system*, is designed to cope with issues that relate to basic survival and to the mechanics of daily living. To optimize the design of this system, a second system, the *deep unconscious system*, deals with emotionally charged issues. After all, if we are upset emotionally or distracted by a conflict in a relationship, our daily functioning can be quite impaired. If the same system had to deal with both survival needs and emotional issues, we would probably be in a state of perpetual chaos.

As you may remember, the survival system makes use of information in very *direct* fashion. The key characteristic of this conscious system is that whatever we think or perceive is processed directly and engenders a direct reaction, sometimes so immediate a reaction that we are in motion before we've even thought about it. A building on fire is a building on fire, and we are moving out of the place almost before we know what we know. If the boss threatens to fire you, you generally know full well, directly and consciously, that the boss is dissatisfied, and that your basic options are to change your work habits, talk to your union representative, or look for a job elsewhere. Not infrequently, in this sort of situation, you can recall a long series of incidents that have led to this moment—incidents that are directly remembered and have been worked over consciously and directly as well. The availability of this information shows that the conscious system has its own unconscious reservoir of directly retrievable memories.

In contrast, there are many perceptions and messages from others whose meaning we simply cannot tolerate in direct, conscious awareness. A small child begins to accumulate evidence that his mother's behavior is unpredictably violent or frighteningly intimate. Perhaps the child begins to realize that a parent at times wishes him harm. Emotionally charged information of this kind, often communicated indirectly and by implication, is, as a rule, too terrifying to bear in awareness. Perceptions of this kind would derail our everyday, conscious functioning. Nonetheless, the information is important if not critical to us, and it must be received and worked over so we can cope.

For each of us, then, there is a system within our minds that receives incoming messages and information subliminally, without direct awareness. This deep unconscious system silently works over and processes the charged information. It sorts out the elements of a hurtful situation, the nature of the threat, and suggests ways of handling the danger. But the information that is being processed is terrifying and cannot be experienced directly by the conscious mind. Because of this, most of the perceptions and working over of this type of potentially disturbing experience are conveyed indirectly through *transformed* or disguised images—such as those that occur in dreams.

It is the conflict between the two systems that accounts for the forgetting of dreams. The conscious system wants no part of the dream experience, manifest or latent. The deep unconscious system wishes, so to speak, to inform. Driven in opposite directions by our two mental systems, the ultimate decision—to remember or to forget—is made well beyond awareness. On the other hand, although we are not in conscious control of this decision, it is possible, as we will see, to increase the likelihood of remembering and keeping available a particular dream experience.

TIMOTHY awoke in the middle of the night, in a state of sexual arousal and realized that he'd been dreaming

> *he is making love to the beautiful female attorney who just joined his law firm.*

In the morning, however, all he could remember was having awakened during the night in a state of arousal. He knew there was a dream connected with his sexual feelings, but try as he may, he was unable to recall its content.

On the simplest level, Timothy was feeling guilty about being so deeply attracted to a married colleague. Equally disturbing was a series of unconscious perceptions that suggested mutual attraction on her part and sexual availability should he wish it. On the most disguised level of this dream, the situation had aroused memories, still unconscious, of several incestuous experiences that had occurred when Timothy was a teenager, between himself and his sister. Timothy's dread of experiencing these images, even in disguise, saw to it that by morning, Timothy had forgotten his dream, though of course its influence—the influence of the underlying and unconscious perceptions and memories—would remain. Timothy would react to the situation with blinders on: He would lack full vision of the issues and memories the relationship was arousing.

GIVEN THE powerful inner mental forces that stand opposed to our remembering our dreams, and given that these forces are almost entirely beyond conscious awareness and control—and modified only slowly at best—what can be done to facilitate dream recall?

First, believe in your dreams and in what they can

deliver. More precisely, believe in yourself as a dreamer. Familiarize yourself with the unique view of yourself and the world conveyed through dreams both directly, and even more so, through disguise. In a very real sense, every dreamer is a genius waiting to be discovered.

As you build faith in yourself as a dreamer, recognize as well the special intelligence and coping capacity that are so beautifully compressed into dreams. Acquiring a perspective on the unique powers embodied in a dream on the one hand, and the dreaded issues with which dreams often ultimately deal on the other, brings with it a kind of yearning to know your dreams—to fish them out from the darkened waters of your sleeping hours at the very moment those waters recede, pulling their contents back out to sea.

Develop, too, a belief in yourself as someone who can tolerate the surprising and usually painful truths that are encoded within dreams. *Recognize that avoiding dreams is tantamount to avoiding the most basic emotional issues in your life.* Your conscious attitude—often without your realizing it—prefers denial and avoidance over awareness and confrontation, mentally if not in actuality. In contrast, the deep unconscious system prefers knowing to not knowing. Thus, decoding your dreams is actually necessary if you want to take on and try to resolve the emotional issues with which you are faced.

The pain that dream knowledge can bring is the price of that knowledge. And even though determination to tolerate that pain is merely conscious, that stance will nonetheless affect the deep unconscious system. That is, faith in the power of dreams to help you to heal your emotional wounds and resolve your emotional conflicts helps make you a high dream recaller.

This book has been designed to give you the perspective you need to want a dream enough to remember it. Reading it will help you develop a general interest in dreams (especially your own), and also promote dream recall. There are, as well, several practical measures that will help you recall your dreams. If you awaken from a dream in the middle of the night (and that is not uncommon), lie back and allow your dream to come close to the surface, where it will be easily accessed by conscious attention. If the dream begins to slip away from you, increase your efforts. Make deliberate attempts to capture and fix into your awareness one or two striking elements of the dream. Often, such elements act like towlines which enable you to pull the dream back toward you, where it can be anchored by fixing its most powerful images in your conscious mind.

Though you are probably quite exhausted and eager to return to sleep, you need to stay awake at least ten minutes to fix the dream in your memory and recall it in the morning. You may be tempted to write the dream down so that it is fixed and preserved, but as I will discuss a bit later, yielding to this temptation is to succumb to the part of your mind that wishes to render the dream sterile and meaningless—to your defensive, rather than your knowing, side. Instead, briefly allow yourself to free-associate to the dream—simply let your thoughts wander in response to the dream images.

Try to remember one or two of the major *triggers* from the preceding day that prompted the dream. Dreams are generally prompted by emotionally charged experiences. Many of these are easily recognized because they are significant experiences consciously; the dream will be working over their less conscious aspects—implications that have not been realized or that are hurtful or disturbing, or extraordinarily gratifying. If you can identify the trigger for a dream, and fix in your half-awake mind a couple of the most compelling dream images, you most likely will remember the dream again on awakening in the morning. Though some images may be lost, you will retain enough of the dream to allow for its *reexpansion* (the waking recall of forgotten or new dream elements), its extension into fresh associated images, and ultimately its analysis.

Similar efforts will help to fix dreams into conscious awareness when you awake in the morning. First, allow yourself to wake up slowly and gradually. As you become more and more awake, use your conscious awareness to scan the images that are beginning to fade from the previous night's sleep. This is a peculiar activity—you're alternating between lying quietly and permitting the dream to enter awareness and then attempting to explore with your conscious attention that fading space in which your dreams transpired. Catch as much of your dream experience as possible, and then lie back and relax for a while. Let your mind wander, but try to avoid any kind of extended thinking about your reality problems. Except for identifying possible triggers from the previous day, preoccupation with the details of real issues are the enemy of dream recall. Fixating on such realities will draw virtually all of the attention of your conscious mind to its accustomed domain—the undisguised and direct meanings of survival issues in waking experience. This will effectively shut down expressions from the deep unconscious system. By avoiding this, you can maintain a kind of reverie state which will increase the chances of capturing dreams.

Lying back and waiting and then actively exploring will very naturally lead to bits of mental wanderings, free associations, and stray thoughts. Often, this will create a context wherein an elusive dream fragment will suddenly pop into awareness. Again pause momentarily and review the conflicts and disturbing incidents of the previous day that are probably triggering your dreams. Dream experiences are organized around these incidents. Identifying them will frequently provide still another path of entry into awareness for a forgotten dream or dream image.

Think of a dream as the proverbial tip of a massive iceberg. By free associating, you are attempting to probe beneath the surface of the water, to get a feel for the formative structure to which the manifest dream is attached. Sometimes, while you're doing this, fragments that are not part of the manifest dream itself, but are part of its underlying structure, will come loose and float to the water's surface.

Once you are out of bed, dreams may suddenly peer at you from around some mental corner, or dart across your mind before you can quite get hold of the content. This usually happens when you are engaged in a relatively automatic activity such as brushing your teeth or riding as a passenger in a car. As the conscious mind relaxes, a state of mind is created that permits the deep unconscious system to press forward even though you are awake. Anything that you do during the day that creates a passive, undirected state of mind also creates room for idle thought, daydreaming, reverie, and stray dream memories. If you want to catch these memories, you need to make an effort. Many times you will simply get a sense of a fleeting image attached to the memory of a feeling—a sense of pleasure or grief or the sense of having been in a particular place or with a particular person. If you don't concentrate on this fragment and try to reel it in, the entire dream will quickly slip into oblivion.

There are a variety of other experiences that may evoke

the recollection of an unremembered or forgotten dream. I call these stimuli *recall residues*, because they are at the opposite pole of reality from *day residues*, the triggers for the dream. Recall residues complete the circle, so to speak, that embeds the dream in the realities of our daily lives. Someone will mention in passing that he or she is planning a ski trip, and suddenly you remember that you had a dream about skiing. This sort of thing happens all the time, but it is often more complex than an apparent memory jog. When a dream memory suddenly surfaces in response to something said by someone else, that someone else is very likely to be of importance to the latent content of the now remembered dream. Such are the webs we weave with dreams and waking reality—so much richer than waking reality alone.

Most of the dreams that come back to you in this way will be freshly dreamed—the night before, or at most, the night before that. However, on occasion you may suddenly remember an old dream—or several. Sometimes remembering a fresh dream begets one from the past, or vice versa. Whenever a dream catches your attention, no matter what the vintage, it is worth getting hold of, because, as a rule, it has some relevance to your current emotional life. It is alive and pertinent, and should be handled accordingly. The motto is simple: Catch any dream in sight, mark it well so it is saved for later recall and exploration, and keep the faith in yourself as dreamer.

THE IDEA OF writing down a dream—to capture it permanently—seems sensible. Why not keep a pad and pencil or tape recorder by your bedside? After all, the goal is to prevent dreams from slipping away, to keep them available so they can eventually be analyzed and understood.

There are many factors that argue against this practice. For one, some people have discovered that the availability of pencil and pad actually diminishes rather than increases dream recall. Their knowing that a dream will be fixed immediately can "frighten the dream away." Remember. that we have defenses against remembering dreams. As you begin to write down a dream, your defenses against recall may simply go into action and you won't be able to remember the dream at all.

There are, of course, many dreamers who do recall and then record their dreams. It could be argued that a re-corded dream is better than no dream at all. However, a recorded dream seldom, if ever, yields to effective dream analysis.

A dream is a highly personal experience, an emotion-ally powerful set of images that you alone are equipped to appreciate and understand fully. More to the point, a dream is a living thing. Interpretation is not equivalent to pressing a dead flower into a book as a keepsake. It is more like transplanting a living shoot from one medium to another. It is still connected to its root system, and it will grow and change in its new domain. Writing down a dream cuts it off from its roots and turns it into a distant art object.

Forgetting a dream is also a natural process; it is not a personal deficit that you need to remedy by keeping a recording device nearby. Unconscious efforts to protect yourself from undue mental/emotional pain are necessary and normal. If you have had a dream that is too painful to bear, too risky to recall, or too dangerous to analyze, you are better off forgetting it than struggling with infor-mation the conscious mind is not ready to accept. When the conscious mind is ready to cope with the meanings embedded in a dream, in most instances, you will dream some other version of it later—and remember it. When you are in a vulnerable state, even well-disguised manifest dream images may be too disturbing to contend with. Why not accept the unconscious wisdom of your own mind and allow the remembering and forgetting of dreams to occur as a natural process? If the efforts described above don't help bring a dream to consciousness and fix it in the mind, then just let it go.

Further, a written dream is removed from the internal flow of conscious and unconscious thinking and imagery in which it must remain in order to retain its depth and its meaning on multiple levels. The necessary play between defensiveness and openness, free association and avoidance, meaning revealed and meaning concealed is entirely sidestepped. What was once a gnawing, inner mental experience in need of resolution is now an external, and essentially dead, foreign body. Because of this, most attempts to analyze or understand the written dream are confined to its surface imagery, a greatly limited domain. Typically, it is difficult to free-associate to the externalized version of the dream, and the much-needed dream/associational network, which gives substance and expansion to surface dream images, fails to materialize. The elusive dream image may well have been captured, but the life has been taken out of it.

The written dream, then, is a dream disowned. Often, the decision to write down a dream is itself motivated by the conflict between recall and meaningful discovery on the one hand, and flight from meaning on the other. One can hardly imagine a better way to effect a compromise that favors the obliteration of the most important levels of meaning in a dream than to do so in the guise of sup-posedly increasing our opportunities for dream analysis. Even when the conscious mind is prepared to accept the meaning of a dream, dream recall is opposed by natural defenses. These defenses are expressed every step of the way—from the actual dream experience to its ultimate in-depth interpretation.

Writing down a dream takes the heart, the guts, the emotions out of the dream, and renders it a distant intel-lectual product. The original ties to the deep unconscious system, so vital to the revelations made when the deepest meanings of dreams are unraveled, are replaced with links to the conscious system of a kind evoked by the external world. Much is lost; little, if anything, is gained. The dreamer becomes a stranger to his or her own dream.

This is similar to what happens when we decide to tell a dream to a friend or to someone we dreamed about. A trained mental health professional may be able to work productively with a reported dream from a client, but the friend or colleague who hears our dream can observe only its surface, and will inevitably bring to bear his or her own associations or intellectual resources. The dream itself with its many vital layers attached to the emotional life of the dreamer becomes an object of "scientific" study or, worse, serves merely as a vehicle for unconscious conflicts cur-rently operating between the dreamer and the listener.

Many dreamworkers, including Freud, have observed that anyone to whom you choose to tell a dream is in some way involved in the unconscious meaning of the dream itself. Furthermore, in the very telling, you may be yielding to a powerful need to use the recipient of the dream as a receptacle for unconscious messages. When this happens, you yourself will almost never be aware of what you have communicated. Nevertheless, the person who has received your messages will have registered them in his or her own deep unconscious system and be under their influence. The situation could well deteriorate into the blind leading the blind, to the disadvantage of both. It is far wiser to check an impulse to tell someone a dream and to privately consider that unfulfilled need as part of your associations to the dream—an element to be analyzed and understood.

DREAMS ARE an effort to communicate and adapt through the expression of meaning. They draw on the almost unlimited capacities of the human mind to adjust to many situations through thought and contemplation, insight and understanding. At the opposite pole to dreams stands reflexive, or blind, action—an adaptive mode well suited to emergency situations, but far less effective when the use of knowledge, anticipation, and mental work is possible. Under those circumstances, thoughtless action often leaves us filled with regrets.

Writing down a dream or telling someone a dream are types of action that interfere with the contemplative adaptive attitude, of which dreams are a part. Often, we sense, without actually knowing consciously, that a dream contains disguised or latent images of potential threat, and we try somehow magically to get rid of the toxic stuff. We shift from thought to an action mode—from associating mentally to the dream to putting it on paper or telling it to someone else. Under the influence of the superficial unconscious system and our needs for immediate protection, we mistakenly believe that we can get rid of the power of the dream images in that way, but the inner conflicts remain with us. And all we have done is complicate the situation by moving ourselves into an action mode and by revealing ourselves to others in ways we do not know and which are, in general, hurtful to them and self-defeating to ourselves.

There is, then, an antithesis between dreaming, imaging, thinking, and exploring on the one hand, and acting under unconscious influence—so-called acting-out—on the other. These are two extreme modes of adaptation, and when we shift gears from thought to blind and unwitting action, we remain in the action mode for some time. Action becomes our way of coping, and thoughts fall by the wayside or, at best, become a secondary factor—mainly a way of rationalizing away the things we have done.

There are occasions when telling a dream to someone else, done as part of sharing dream experiences, will foster peaceful interaction among the dream tellers and serve a communal purpose. This kind of dream telling is constructive, but rare in present-day societies. Those of us who are interested in using dream analysis as a personal resource must recognize that there is a difference between a culture that values the communal self over the individual self and our own culture, which fosters an arsenal of personal defenses that operate under the guise of fostering communal harmony. Moreover, a less self-oriented culture will not be dealing with the same kinds of unconscious conflicts that attend the development of an autonomous self.

Only the dreamer can interpret his or her dream. A sensitive professional may help a dreamer to focus, but only the dreamer can experience or fathom a dream's deepest meanings. Everyone can take guesses, and a perceptive observer may sometimes hit the mark, but almost without exception, these gratuitous interpretations are personally motivated and biased. Such insights are intellectualizations, and although they may seem clever, they almost always lead the dreamer astray, compromising his or her own relationship to the dream elements.

MARK AND CELIA are a young couple who live together. Celia is divorced and has a four-year-old daughter. Her ex-husband, Ted, had had some major business setbacks, and though he was still supporting his ex-wife and child, he often disappeared for months at a time. When he did resurface, he usually had dinner with Celia to discuss their daughter and whatever problems had come up, and usually took the opportunity to give Celia some extra money—at times quite large sums. Mark had objected both to these liaisons and to Celia's accepting the money.

One night Celia told Mark that she would not be able to have dinner with him the following evening as planned because Ted was in town and it was the only time he could see her. Mark accepted the situation with resignation, but he was then impotent with Celia in bed that night.

The following morning, Mark awakened with the memory of a dream of getting married, but the rest seemed blurred. Curious, he lay back for a while and reached out mentally toward the dream. Some dream images began to form in his mind: of being in a hotel room where he must get dressed for the wedding; of guests arriving, preventing him from having sex with someone; of having only a brown suit to wear and wondering if it is appropriate for a wedding; and of not being certain who he is marrying.

How interesting, Mark thought, as he turned to Celia, who had been awake for a while. "I had this crazy dream about getting married," he said, and told her the sequence of events as he remembered them. But Celia was irritated and felt insulted by the dream; she felt that it indicated some sort of ambivalence about their relationship—he didn't know who he was marrying, he wanted to make love, but he was interrupted by the arrival of a third party. She asked immediately if the wedding guests were supposed to be Ted, given their own failed attempt to make love the night before. Mark was startled by the question and denied that the dream had anything to do with Ted. He also claimed, rather lamely, that the dream must mean that he wanted to marry Celia, but the discussion went nowhere and the conversation was dropped.

Later that afternoon, without giving the matter much thought, Mark arranged to have dinner with a female colleague to talk about a mutual project. As the evening wore on, however, he began to realize that he was quite attracted to this woman, and that he was being unusually seductive. He found himself suggesting that they go back to her apartment for coffee. Once in the street, however, on the point of hailing a cab, he thought better of the idea. Why am I doing this? he said to himself; I've never been unfaithful to Celia. Why should I start now?

Let's take a look at this situation in terms of the dream Mark shared with Celia. Obviously, Mark felt that Celia was being insensitive to him in remaining socially involved with her former husband. And he was justified in feeling that Celia's breaking their date to have dinner with Ted was a form of blind action; as it turned out, other arrangements would have been possible—arrangements that would not have disturbed Celia's plans with Mark. On the other hand, Mark himself had shifted into a blind action mode, answering Celia's insensitivity with impotence. Rather than discussing the situation with her, he expressed his anger toward Celia by a form of withholding. Had he associated to his dream the following morning, he might have come to terms with what he was feeling.

But Mark was apparently incapable of shifting to a contemplative, thoughtful mode. He continued to act by telling Celia his dream. As a result, the dream was discharged, removed from Mark's inner mental struggles, subjected to a bit of intellectualized guesswork, and discarded. The action mode continued when Mark arranged to have dinner with his colleague and exploited the underlying chemistry in their working relationship.

By telling Celia the dream, Mark precluded free-associating to and analyzing it. In the telling, the deeper meanings of the dream became inaccessible. Each brief effort Mark made to associate to his dream led nowhere. Though we may wish it to be otherwise, when a dream is told to someone else this shutting-down effect usually occurs.

Looking at Mark's dream in light of its waking-life triggers—the problems between himself and Celia—suggests that the dream portrayed and disguised Mark's anger with Celia because he unconsciously perceived her as being unfaithful to him with Ted. The dream images suggest that Mark did see Ted as an intruder, that he had wishes to leave Celia or to be unfaithful to her (as well as to marry her), and that his impotency was indeed a reaction to Ted's presence. It might be objected that Celia's conjecture was basically correct, but the point is that by telling Celia the dream, Mark was using the dream as a weapon against her, and her reaction was, understandably, to feel angry and hurt and to fling the unconscious meaning of his images back at him. Mark was neither free nor prepared to integrate her interpretation into his own thinking.

Had Mark free-associated to the dream himself and

realized some of what he was feeling, he might have been able to talk to Celia about the situation and to work out things more peaceably. This would have precluded the blind-action response that had brought him close to initiating an otherwise pointless sexual encounter with his colleague.

I'VE STATED that only the dreamer knows the meanings of his or her dream, but this knowledge is not packaged in straightforward fashion with direct and immediately accessible information. Instead, it is transformed—disguised or encoded—so that the dreamer both knows and does not know. Changing the not-knowing into knowing is the substance of dream interpretation. Capturing the dream is a good beginning, but it may lead to a blind alley—as we saw with Mark. But there is more: As it turns out, the captured dream is only half a dream or less. There is a vital second stage in re-creating a dream so that it exists in all its fullness. Until you have reached that point, you shouldn't begin to analyze.

7
CREATING A DREAM
OF SUBSTANCE

MOST PEOPLE think that a dream happens entirely during sleep, and that we merely remember it the following morning, but it is more complicated than that. Very early in his studies, Freud suggested that we don't actually remember the dream as dreamed; the waking mind is unwittingly changing it while remembering—making sense of the images, imposing a logical structure on the action. The remembered dream, then, is a mixture of the actual dream experience and inevitable unconscious alterations that occur when we awaken and recall the dream, fixing it in awareness. It is this product of the sleeping and waking states that we call a dream.

Once remembered, a dream is usually frozen as such, although at times it will fade away in part or in entirety or, more rarely, will be recovered in fragments or embellished in the course of an ensuing day.

These remembered images, fraught with meaning, Freud termed the *manifest dream*. Anything that exists beyond the surface of the dream he considered to be *associations* to the dream. The dreamer's associations are not just an important supplement—they are actually vital to the dream experience.

Think of a dream as created in two stages: one during sleep, the other while awake. The first stage is Freud's manifest dream—the dream as dreamed by night and remembered in the morning. The second stage of dream formation occurs by day through associating to the manifest dream and to each of its elements. It is this second-stage effort that creates the total dream. It is by this means alone that a dream is completed and revealed in its full complexity and with all its force.

In other words, the manifest dream is half a dream, or less. A full dream is a *dream/associational network,* and this network is the closest we can get to a total dream experience. Because we have many natural defenses against total dream recall, the temptation is always to limit a dream to the manifest dream remembered, and to forgo the associational process. Many books on dream interpretation deride this process of free association as "Freudian" and unnecessarily complicated, as though the method were somehow deliberately intended to discourage popular dream analysis and restrict it to psychoanalysts.

It is unfortunate that psychoanalytic thought lends itself to this kind of unwitting resistance to meaning. Often a classically psychoanalytic interpretation of a dream is a cliché or a caricature of emotionally pertinent information. (One thinks of the old one-liner: "Oedipus, shmedipus—just as long as you love your mother!") Yet, paradoxically, the more you restrict yourself to the dream as immediately remembered, the more likely you are to confine yourself precisely to a clichéd, intellectualized, fundamentally hollow interpretation.

THINK OF AN amoeba just beneath the surface of the water. Its main body is divided into five compartments, each sending out a little leg or pseudopod to the water's surface. If you were to take a microscope and observe the amoeba from above, at the surface layer you would see five little legs, each with its own shape, together making up a kind of pattern. If you were to stop at this point, you would not know very much about the amoeba. You would know something about the amoeba's offshoots, but you would entirely miss the fact that they are connected to the main body of the amoeba, and you would know nothing at all about the basic structure of the whole entity. The only way to fully appreciate the amoeba from the perspective of the water's surface would be to trace down each of the little legs to its presumed body segment. Then you would have to integrate the body and its parts into a whole. Only that sort of effort would give you a relatively complete picture of the organism.

A dream has a similar structure. The pseudopods that reach the surface are the manifest elements of a dream, or the dream as dreamed. Even if you were to examine these manifest elements closely, you would still be looking at the dream's offshoots, the pattern of the dream images. But each of these images extends beneath the surface of the dream to an interconnected network of additional dream material. And it is the manifest dream, together with these underlying components, that constitutes and completes the body of a dream experience. Clearly, the surface story has a shape of its own, but its relationship to the whole dream entity is not immediately apparent, and its meaning cannot be appreciated without some effort to understand what its various components are connected to.

As a rule, each surface component of a dream calls forth a host of associations. Even if you are accustomed to thinking about the memories and feelings and thoughts evoked by various dream images, you probably separate the manifest dream from this associational complex; nonetheless the manifest dream is continuous with these underlying associations. The associations to an image, however remote they may seem, should be considered part of your dream. In a completed dream analysis the underlying themes of a dream carry far more meaning than the manifest dream elements themselves.

You need to think of the dream and your associations to it as a single complex of dream material. This complex of both direct and encoded reactions is actually a unified reaction to the emotionally charged triggers that set the dreaming process into motion. Indeed, the deep unconscious system responds silently and extensively to these triggers, and its activities are reflected both in the dream as recalled and in the dream associations. The dream as remembered, then, is but a small part of the total dream experience. A dream must be completed by allowing time for loose and unencumbered associations to as much of the surface dream as possible. We can then treat the entire dream/associational network as a single dream event, and analyze it accordingly. The result of this approach is far richer than the formulations derived from work with the remembered dream alone.

Free associating is something of an art. It can be done during any free interlude and involves unencumbered thinking that is undirected, loose, and without evident purpose. Free association usually has a point of departure, such as the total dream, the dream's literal meaning, a particular dream element, or even an association to a dream that has already occurred to you. Be passive and open—and allow for surprise. The more relaxed your general state of mind, the wider the range of associations and the more

complete the total dream. Especially suited to gaining this
is free associating in bed or while lying down, preferably
in the dark so that outside distractions are minimized.

When you remember a dream in the morning, you
should set aside some time for at least a brief period of
loose, open associating in response to one or another of
the elements of the remembered dream. You should allow
as well for intermittent periods where you permit any
thought at all to enter into your awareness. Only after
performing this kind of unencumbered association should
you take stock. The associational complex should emerge
as spontaneously as possible and in a state of consciousness
relatively close to the sleeping state—something like the
state of consciousness that occurs when one is just beginning to fall asleep and thoughts, daydreams, and reverie
begin to blur.

The advantage of beginning to complete the dream/
associational network in the morning is that it is then
available for additional associating, and even for brief periods of dream analysis as moments during the day permit.
Failing that, wait for a quiet moment in the evening to
engage in the free-associational activity. But remember
that this is only the first step in an effort that eventually
reaches its climax through the work of trigger decoding.
It is, as we will see, often through free associating that the
most critical triggers for our dreams are discovered. Remember, too, that even if an associational complex has
been created early in the day, an additional period of free
associating is helpful when you begin the dream analysis.

It is sometimes difficult to know how far to pursue an
associational network. You should concentrate on the main
elements of a dream, but you need to be wary of losing
the seemingly unimportant detail whose underlying struc-

ture is actually massive and critical. Psychological defenses and resistances directed against a proper deciphering of a dream operate continuously, and there is no assured approach to associating to and synthesizing a set of dream/associational images. It is best to keep an open mind, and to leave no stone unturned or unanalyzed.

ANDREW AWOKE one morning and remembered dreaming

   he has cancer.

Here is a dream with one pseudopod, a single surface element. As such, it is relatively barren. What would you do with this image? You might start with its literal reference point and ask whether the dream was an accurate perception: Did Andrew have cancer in waking life? Did the dream reflect an unconscious premonition? Perhaps Andrew was attempting to punish himself unconsciously. Or was something "eating him up"? At best, you can only speculate—by substituting a technical term like "masochism" for a blatantly physical dream image, or by playing with words. Standing on its own, the image offers little in the way of understanding.

The dream was sufficiently disturbing to prompt Andrew to work with it a bit. He began to free-associate as he lay in bed, starting from the standpoint of the dream's literal meaning. Andrew knew that he felt perfectly healthy and did not have cancer. He didn't know anyone who had cancer. He thought about his friends, his relatives. One of his uncles was quite on in years and suffering from the effects of advanced diabetes. It was almost as though the excessive sugar in his system were eating away at his body.

Andrew thought about the strain of diabetes in his family. He had managed to escape somehow, but his daughter, Melissa, had not. The day before had been Melissa's birthday. Andrew had felt unhappy and guilty, thinking about the kind of future she was likely to have; but Melissa had been excited and talkative, and after a while he had become distracted by her cheery stories about herself and her grade-school friends.

This is as far as Andrew needed to go with his associations. Undoubtedly, this dream has other underlying tracks, since manifest dream elements virtually always represent more than one set of themes, associations, and meanings. However, Andrew had sufficiently completed his dream to begin to understand an important component of its underlying meanings. Indeed, at times, developing the associations of a dream is tantamount to its interpretation.

Notice that Andrew's dream as dreamed—that he had cancer—evoked only general speculation about illness, self-punishment, and the various emotional metaphors to which the idea of cancer will lend itself. Andrew's associational network, on the other hand, moved in a clear, specific, and richly meaningful direction. The trigger for Andrew's dream was the occasion of his daughter's birthday—the kind of anniversary that typically activates the deep unconscious system. And although Andrew felt concerned about his daughter consciously and felt helpless and unhappy about her illness, he had no awareness of the intensity and scope of his feelings and of their power to influence him. Nor was he aware of the strength of his guilt, which was experienced far more clearly in the deep unconscious part of his mind.

Andrew's dream/associational network indicates a rescue fantasy. By contracting cancer, he, in essence, was offering himself as a substitute for his suffering daughter. It is only in the deep unconscious system that Andrew dared allow an encoded perception of the awful future that may well lie ahead of her—this represented by Andrew's association to his uncle. And it was only in his deep unconscious system that Andrew could experience his view of the diabetes as a devouring cancer—an illness for which he felt so totally responsible that he wished to punish himself through self-destruction. Suddenly Andrew was able to understand the reasons behind an uncharacteristic error that he had made the previous day in his dealings with an important client, which had resulted in his partner's fury and his own feelings of humiliation and pain—it had been an unconscious invitation for punishment.

We can see, then, the extent to which a dream as dreamed needs completing if it is to become a dream accessible to full interpretation. The themes of devouring, self-punishment, and illness were entirely available from the manifest dream elements, but these themes had no specific connection to Andrew. Thus, no matter how rich and extended its elements, a manifest dream by itself remains an isolated, somewhat cold entity. Andrew could have "tried on" these manifest implications in a clichéd, intellectualized fashion, wondering whether he was feeling "devoured" by someone or was experiencing himself as damaged or helplessly attacked. But such formulations have no functional meaning; they are unrelated to a real life with real relationships and real feelings. A completed dream, by contrast—that is, a dream/associational network—is a richly complex whole that is far more substantial than the manifest dream alone, and far more informative if properly decoded. Andrew didn't need to "try on" implications derived from the symbols;

his associations *informed* the symbols and gave them substance and meaning directly pertinent to what he knew and felt in waking life.

TO SAMPLE some of the complexities underlying seemingly innocuous manifest dream elements, we may consider the dream of Cheryl, a single woman in her early thirties. She awakened one morning and remembered a dream in which

> *William Hurt, the actor, is stroking her neck.*

Cheryl is a busy woman with little time for free associating in the morning. Besides, the dream was rather pleasant, and seemed to reflect little more than a passing fantasy. Cheryl had just seen William Hurt on television the night before, accepting an Academy Award for his role in the movie *Kiss of the Spider Woman.*

Much to her surprise, Cheryl felt depressed that day; she was unable to identify a suitable reason for her sluggishness and sense of letdown. Still feeling morbid, she took some time that evening to complete her dream.

Among her associations to William Hurt was Cheryl's present boyfriend, whose name was also William. Her boyfriend was an amateur actor. All of this seemed too obvious; had William in some way "hurt" her? What did this have to do with stroking her neck? Cheryl found herself thinking about the idea of a "spider woman," which led to childhood memories of a character from old vampire movies called the spiderman—a madman who believed that consuming the blood of insects would confer immortality. He considered spiders to be particularly rich with life because spiders consumed flies, and flies consumed other insects. This peculiar line of thought led Cheryl in a number of directions.

For one thing, it made her think about the fact that vampires sink their teeth into the necks of their victims and drain them of blood. She also remembered that her father had at one time been a minor character actor in old B movies. This memory alerted her to the connection the dream was making between her boyfriend and her father.

Cheryl then thought about her father's recent bouts of alcoholism and his mistreatment of her mother. Her mother had been attempting to deny the situation and often dismissed her husband as nothing more than "a pain in the neck." Cheryl immediately saw the bridge between this colloquialism and her dream image, and thought it curious: The dream image represented the actor's contact with her neck as comforting and arousing, whereas the actor's name carried the idea of "pain." Again, she thought about her boyfriend, William. Perhaps something that seemed superficially pleasurable in the relationship with William was unconsciously linked in her mind with her father's behavior toward her mother.

She thought about the fact that William had recently broken a date with her, and she considered the possibility that their relationship in general had become a drain on her emotions. Quite suddenly she recalled an incident at a party the week before. She had been talking to a friend while William moved in and out of various circles of people they knew, and out of the corner of her eye, she saw him kidding around with an old girlfriend. It had been a very momentary gesture—he had put his hand on her neck and bent down to whisper something in her ear, and they had both laughed. Cheryl had felt jealous and angry, but hadn't wanted to make an issue of it, lest she find herself embroiled in a fruitless argument in which William accused her of being possessive and immature. It occurred to her now that she felt more than jealous and angry; she felt abused and exploited. She decided that she had been tolerating the situations with her father and with William to her own detriment; she needed to talk both with her mother and with William.

It also occurred to Cheryl that there were other destructive situations in her life that she had been tolerating silently. Recently, a coworker named Edna had been subtly undermining her position at their firm—in the language of the dream, she was after Cheryl's neck: She wanted Cheryl's job, and she was pretending friendship while attempting to make Cheryl look bad. Spider woman, indeed, Cheryl thought. Edna also had the habit of rubbing her neck when she was tense. Cheryl had always been fond of Edna and she had been trying to overlook her behavior, but on the day of the dream, Edna had quite deliberately gotten Cheryl into trouble and Cheryl had felt drained and depressed by the experience.

We need not further pursue these underlying networks of images and meanings represented by these two relatively simple dream elements—William Hurt and neck stroking. Here, too, the manifest dream alone seems pale and constricted when compared to the associational network. And here, too, the dream was not complete until the associations were allowed to unfold.

A full and meaningful dream analysis, then, depends on having a full and complete dream: The first part is the dream remembered, and the second, the dream associated. An entire dream, fully associated to and waiting for analysis, is easily better than most known ways for gaining access both to the darker and the more creative aspects of the mind.

8

THE SURFACE OF
THE DREAM

WHEN analyzing a dream, it is usually best to proceed from the surface to the depths—from the manifest dream to its latent contents. Before you examine the manifest content of a dream, you should first create a dream/associational network. But if you are pressed for time or want to analyze a dream briefly, carefully examine the *manifest content* of your dream; that is, the surface dream as you remember it—the direct and immediate dream story and images. Martin dreams, for example, that

> *he rescues a young boy who has driven his car into a river.*

The evident themes of the manifest dream involve a young boy, an act of rescue, driving a car into a river, and the danger of drowning. To gain insight from a manifest dream, Martin would have to identify each of these themes, and then try to understand their ramifications.

Ideally, the analysis of a manifest dream is straightforward. You look over the surface elements, acknowledge the cast of characters and the nature of their transactions, and take note of the setting and other aspects of the dream's configuration. In this way, you, as the dreamer, come to realize that these are your issues, your concerns. Simply recognizing them is often meaningful.

The manifest content of Martin's dream was that of a young boy out of control, drowning. This powerful theme seemed to involve the danger of death, and perhaps the loss of a child. On the other hand, he had undone these possibilities by rescuing the boy. Whatever the issue of death and dying evident in these surface themes, Martin felt reassured that he had been able to combat successfully this possibility or concern.

The dream's sequence of events, the ultimate outcome of these events, the indications of coping or failing to cope— all of this is revealed by concentrating our attention on the surface of a dream. Even though this kind of analysis deals only with direct and unencoded images, because they are fished up from the sleeping state they will likely offer a fresh viewpoint on your life situation—however limited that viewpoint may be. As we have been discovering chapter by chapter, the deep unconscious system greatly shapes the manifest content of the dream, so even the surface level of a dream can give you insight into concerns and issues that do not appear in the course of your waking thoughts.

It is also true, however, that an analysis of the manifest content of a dream is a little like Stanley discovering a village where Livingston had been some months earlier. He will certainly find evidence of the time Livingston spent in the village, and he may learn a great deal about the man, but the information does not satisfy the ultimate motive for pursuit—direct contact. Stanley would examine the clues to Livingston's presence not only to understand more about him, but also to determine where he went from there.

So, too, with a manifest dream. At some critical point, you must recognize that the manifest dream is a way station that points to meanings both deeper and more difficult to access. It is easier, of course, to stop at the manifest level. Even psychoanalysts do that. But there can be no ultimate fulfillment of a dream analysis with only a surface interpretation, although it does help us to move into the deeper levels of the dream.

CHESTER dreams that

> he is in a Minnesota farmhouse. He is being held by kidnappers and is trying to escape. He recognizes the house as Celeste's, a woman he has recently stopped seeing. Donna, his present girlfriend, hangs up the telephone when he calls her. Chester feels frustrated and furious with Donna. He is enraged that she doesn't understand the danger he is in.

Here, then, is a manifest dream that we can make use of in two basic ways:

1. As a source of information, and as a means of discovering unnoticed or unrealized insights with respect to yourself, others, and your emotional issues.

2. As a point of departure for free association when you are building a dream/associational network. A dreamer may simply take the surface elements of a dream and associate to them. A more concentrated study of these surface contents and their implications will provide new impressions

122 DECODING YOUR DREAMS

and realizations that can then serve as nodal points for still further ideas and images.

Here, we will concentrate on the first—examining the manifest images of a dream as a way of obtaining immediate information and insight about waking-life situations. You can do this either by exploring the surface of the dream in somewhat splendid isolation or by looking at the dream with some general sense of its particular context. You can stay with the concrete surface of the dream or you can garner further knowledge from the implications that may be directly extracted from the dream images.

Let's look at Chester's dream through the eyes of its creator, who is thirty years old and single.

When Chester studied his dream line by line, he realized first that the site of his dream scenario was a farmhouse Celeste owned. So, Celeste was somehow on his mind, even though he had not given her even a passing thought the previous day—or recently for that matter. Assuming that there are fewer barriers against thinking about someone or something while asleep than while awake, Chester notes that Celeste is on his mind, and wonders why.

Answering this question would lead him into a sequence of free associations, or figuring out the possible context of his dream. Such reflections are the usual response to dream images. In a sense, it is not really possible to look directly at a manifest dream and simply extract evident meanings and implications from it.

In this instance, however, Chester was attempting, as a kind of disciplined exercise, to stay with the manifest elements of his dream and to look at them in sequence. In the next image, he was being held by kidnappers and was trying to escape.

Here, too, Chester was at first surprised by the image. By day, he could remember having no thoughts about kidnapping or criminals. But then he recalled having read about a recent kidnapping in which the victim was inadvertently murdered. It also occurred to him that kidnapping implied entrapment. Putting this idea together with Celeste was not difficult: Celeste had certainly been entrapping and overwhelming in the course of their relationship. In a sense, in leaving Celeste, Chester had escaped from this entrapment. So again, he wondered, why now? Why dream of being kidnapped at Celeste's place and trying to escape when the escape had already been accomplished? He asked himself whether he might somehow harbor a secret wish to return to Celeste. Perhaps he was reminding himself as a kind of warning of the way things used to be.

You can see that Chester is managing to ask more questions than find answers in his analysis of the dream's surface elements. Readings of the manifest contents of dreams are our most speculative responses to dream material, because such an investigation is lacking in both context and extended associations. As an initial step in dream analysis, however, analyzing the dream's surface elements is invaluable.

Returning to his dream, Chester noted that he had turned to Donna for help by calling her from the farmhouse. So Donna, too, was on Chester's mind, and indicated that his relationship with women was of concern to him. He thought about the image of Donna hanging up the phone. Her action implied abandonment, rejection, turning a deaf ear, unavailability, and perhaps hostility. These implications brought to mind an incident that took place with Donna on the night prior to Chester's dream. Chester had made several mindless comments that Donna had been quick to criticize as misogynist and arrogant.

Donna's anger was so vehement that it had caught him off guard. At the time, he figured he had hit a nerve of some sort, and that his best strategy was to apologize and let the incident go. But now, Chester saw that his reaction to the situation was actually more than he could tolerate consciously; his reaction had been so powerful that it hadn't registered in awareness but was being worked over in his unconscious mind.

Chester remembered having felt embarrassed and irritated, but he had eventually shrugged off the exchange as a matter of his thoughtlessness and Donna's hypersensitivity. But now he saw in the final moments of his dream the evidence of inner rage. He realized that rage had been his true reaction, because something in him had shut off after the incident: He had closed himself off to Donna, and he had numbed himself against his feelings for fear of their power. He saw that this was another meaning of the image of Donna hanging up the telephone. He blamed her for the loss of contact between them after the incident. So even the manifest dream bore witness to feelings he could not allow himself to recognize in waking life.

A bit of synthesis is now possible. In his anger with Donna, Chester was unconsciously reminded of the relationship with Celeste—his feeling that he was being controlled, that he was being trapped by somebody else's ideas of how to live a life, being forced to live, so to speak, in someone else's conceptual house, amid someone else's ideological furniture, deprived of his freedom to be what he was without censure—and in some danger of being inadvertently killed in the process. He had been expecting Donna to rescue him from these feelings, and she hadn't, and Chester's rage evidently led him to consider cutting Donna out of his life entirely and going back into the old situation with Celeste. The dream was warning him that exercising this option would only reignite the sense of entrapment he'd escaped when he'd broken up with Celeste.

Much of this had failed to reach Chester's awareness on the night prior to the dream. A careful look at the manifest dream and its implications gave Chester significant insight into the reactions he had repressed. He saw now that he had withdrawn from Donna, and that he might express his anger at some inappropriate or irrational moment. With the knowledge drawn from his manifest dream, Chester was better able to cope with his current feelings toward her.

IN EXTRACTING meaning from the surface of a dream, use a simple checklist. This strategy does have the disadvantage of turning the dream into a narrative that has a beginning, middle, and end, whereas the meaning of a dream is usually better understood when it is seen in overview. On the other hand, an overview is not useful unless you have carefully looked at some of the details of a dream. In Chester's dream, for example, being trapped by kidnappers in Celeste's farmhouse is followed by an angry exchange and loss of contact with Donna. One might say that in waking life, the sequence of events happened the other way around: anger and withdrawal from Donna precipitated a series of unconscious reactions, which led to memories of being entrapped by Celeste. But, in fact, the dream has its own emotional agenda. Although the conscious mind remembers the dream as a series of narrative events, the emotions embodied by the dream images are really happening all at the same time: the feeling of entrapment, the desire to go back to Celeste, the memory of how it actually was with Celeste, the rage and disbelief over Donna's behavior, the need to cut off his contact with her—all of this is part of a complex pattern of emotional response to a trigger situation. It is one reaction—with many aspects.

In trying to analyze a dream as an all-at-once reaction, however, the dream's inner emotional logic seldom becomes apparent until you have gone through the images step by step. So, initially, you do need to examine the manifest dream as a sequence of images, but you also need to keep yourself from getting stuck in this step-by-step perspective. You need to let it go once you have extracted the necessary information from it.

1. The cast of characters—who is involved in the dream?

Chester's dream involved Celeste (by virtue of being in her farmhouse), Donna, some kidnappers, and himself. Chester determined from their presence that Celeste and Donna were both on his mind in some way. His own presence in his dream told him that his relationship with each of them was at issue—in need of working over. The kidnappers are ill-defined, and since Chester knows no such person or persons directly, they are more a carrier of meaning and point of departure for additional associations than an indicator of a direct, interpersonal issue.

Often, the people involved in a dream are the backbone of its manifest meanings and implications. Keeping in mind that your search, ultimately, is for unnoticed concerns and problems, the appearance of someone in a dream image should lead you to scrutinize both your current and past relationship with that person.

2. Study the manifest *themes* of a dream.

The themes of a dream carry a substantial portion of its meaning. Here, too, the search is for the unknown, unrecognized, and repressed. And again, these will be matters of concern, need, and perception. Often, the realization of a thematic issue will bring into focus an emotional problem that has been missed or neglected by the conscious system. Once discovered, the overlooked issues may seem self-evident or almost trivial to an outside observer. But the person who has experienced an emotionally charged situation and has either blunted its implications or remained unaware of its existence often reacts to his or her discovery with considerable amazement. It is in the immediate moment of discovering the obvious, in realizing how the conscious system has covered over or minimized an active or potential threat, that one begins to fathom the power of our conscious, defensive needs. All the more reason to draw upon the perceptions we allow ourselves to express in our dreams.

It is important to identify as many as possible of the themes in a manifest dream. Chester might easily have overlooked one detail of his dream—that it placed him in a farmhouse in Minnesota—and its thematic implications, because the image of being kidnapped and trying to escape was so much more powerful. (It was Freud who warned us that dreams have an investment system of their own, one that is often far different from what we stress on a conscious, waking level.) Seemingly minor details suggest thematic threads in a manifest dream that not infrequently are the container of powerful unrecognized meanings.

3. Make note of the setting of the dream, both for what it reveals directly and as a stimulus for further associations.

There is often a close interweaving between a study of who appears in a dream, the nature of all detectable themes, and the locale of a dream. We have already seen that the farmhouse in Chester's dream had begun to evoke important associations and realizations in him. As he continued to associate, the blending of these three components of his manifest dream became even more evident.

Minnesota is Chester's home state. Through associations, this image, a mixture of setting and theme, would conjure up a host of subsidiary themes—all part of the deeper structure of the dream. Chester also recalled reading a news story about a man in Minnesota who had murdered his girlfriend. This memory underscored his association to the kidnappers who had inadvertently murdered their victim. Chester's manifest dream accompanied by a minimum of association indicates how far the depth of his rage—not only at Donna's current behavior, but probably at Celeste's past behavior—went beyond his conscious experience. As we have seen, it is typical of the deep unconscious system to experience and react with raw emotions that are far more powerful than the feelings we are aware of in waking experience.

The farmhouse Chester initially saw as belonging to Celeste, he realized, was a combination of her house and the farmhouse that belonged to his grandparents. He remembered their house as a place of warmth and comfort and protection. In thinking about it, Chester experienced his deep longings for a wife and family, longings that were somehow being spoiled by his failed relationships with women. He began to wonder whether he had been blaming Donna and Celeste for his own sense of defeat; perhaps his own inner needs were leading him to choose women who would eventually disappoint him.

In general, you should treat the themes of a dream as applicable to yourself, as well as to the other figures in the manifest dream. This is true at every level of dream interpretation. In tapping the manifest images of a dream, notice all possible meanings and ramifications, seeking a relatively unguarded and incisive view of yourself and others, your life situation, and how well you are coping with it—and by what means. As you review each component of a dream—its people, themes, and the like—try to move from single, isolated impressions to the creation of a whole—an overall view of your personal universe at the moment.

As Chester recognized that he had combined his grandparents' farmhouse and Celeste's, he also saw that he was expressing the contradiction between his ideal for a relationship and what he was experiencing in reality. It occurred to him that the tension and distress he had experienced with Celeste was not unlike some of what he had been feeling recently while staying at Donna's apartment. An impression began to take shape—perhaps he had been more unhappy lately in the relationship with Donna than he'd been aware of.

The image of Donna hanging up on his desperate phone call clearly indicated a feeling of having tried to communicate and being shut out. Chester's responsive anger was quite straightforward, mainly tapping a well of feelings he had suppressed by day.

4. Examine how well and with what means the people in the dream are coping.

Dreams are by no means slides or still pictures. They involve activities of the mind that are responsive to recent events; they are part of our efforts to cope. For this reason, you want to develop more than a static picture of the elements of a dream; you want to weave these elements into a picture that tells you something about the issues at hand and how you are dealing with them—and with what degree of success or failure. This will alert you to situations in waking life in which you are feeling overwhelmed and unable to cope, but will also tell you where you are managing better than you were.

In Chester's dream, he is trying to escape his kidnappers and to elicit Donna's help. She turns away from him, leaving him angered and in danger. In other words, Chester is trying to extricate himself from a difficult situation but is failing to do so. In simple terms, we call this a *failure in coping*. Recognizing his lack of success in handling the dream situation helped Chester realize that he had not been able to resolve his mixed feelings toward Donna and that he did not know how to handle the repercussions of their most recent argument. As he worked with his dream, Chester came to acknowledge, if nothing else, his lack of resolution. He was now in a position to think out possible alternatives, and in time, to do something constructive and effective about the growing crisis with Donna.

NOW WE will look at Adrienne's dream and go through the same steps. Adrienne dreamed that

> *a man breaks into her bedroom. He tries to murder her by suffocating her with her pillow. She pushes him off and tries to kill him with a knife hidden under the blanket. Another man appears unannounced and forces the intruder to leave.*

Beginning with the manifest level of this dream, Adrienne first looked at the cast of characters. She realized that the intruder resembled a character actor she had seen in a movie the night before, playing a violent criminal. The other man in the dream—the one who took the intruder away—was not familiar to her. But he was wearing a sport jacket that reminded her of one her father had owned when she was a child. As she was thinking about that, she realized that the jacket was also similar to one worn by Dennis, an attractive and supportive man she'd started dating recently.

The trigger for a dream seldom appears in the manifest contents of the dream; therefore, if you are confining yourself to an analysis of these manifest contents, begin describing the dream with the words: "For some reason . . ." (i.e., for reason of an unknown trigger). For example, Adrienne began her analysis of the dream by saying, "For some reason, I dreamed about two men, one who tried to murder me, and one who saved and protected me."

Although Adrienne was focusing on the manifest level of her dream, she could not overlook the connection between the image of the intruder and the fact that her apartment had been burglarized two nights earlier. Adrienne had returned home to find that the place had been broken into, and her television and several other valuable articles had been stolen. Although the dream scenario is not heavily disguised, the details are different from what they were in reality—in the dream, the intruder breaks into Adrienne's bedroom while she is asleep, whereas in the actual situation she had not been at home at the time of the break-in. Adrienne's new boyfriend, Dennis, had already been a source of comfort to Adrienne in waking life, and she was not surprised by the role he played in her dream (by association to the man's jacket). And she was pleased by the connection the dream made between Dennis and her father, because she had not consciously realized that in many important ways both men had shown similar strengths. This was a surprise to Adrienne and an important insight as well.

Adrienne, of course, recognized the setting of the dream as her apartment, and saw it as an indication that she was still working through and trying to resolve her reactions and feelings to the burglary. The themes speak strongly to this issue, in their inclusion of a break-in, attempted murder, suffocation, revenge with a knife, and the emergence of a protector who steps in and defuses the situation. The image of suffocation tied in for Adrienne with the asthmatic attack she had suffered after discovering her burglarized apartment. Overall, the dream images expressed in raw form Adrienne's sense of having been violated by the real intruder—to the point of feeling assaulted and nearly destroyed. In talionic fashion, the deep unconscious system spoke of vengeance in kind—along with wishes for retrospective rescue, and the need to deal somehow with the situation less violently.

Prior to the dream, Adrienne had not consciously experienced the full measure of her sense of assault and wish for vengeance. The manifest dream expressed these feelings with great clarity. But what now of the sequence of the dream? In this instance, there was first an attack, then defense and a near battle to the death. But the dream ended on a peaceful note when a man stepped in and simply removed the intruder. Clearly this sequence of events was constructive. Adrienne could draw from this aspect of her dream a reassurance that her sense of having been violated and of wishing to do violence was under control; she was

moving toward less costly and disruptive ways of dealing
with her recent trauma. Had the sequence been reversed—
a peaceful attempt to remove the intruder followed by a
violent battle—Adrienne would have been well-advised to
see the dream as a warning that her inner self and state
were not at peace, and that she was far from resolving her
perceptions of the situation and her reactions to it.

Constructive sequences, then, that move from uncontrolled and chaotic images to those with greater control
and more order and organization suggest, but do not guar-
antee, movement toward a suitable adaptation to a particular trauma situation. On the other hand, a so-called
regressive sequence, in which there is an increasing sense
of turmoil, destruction, and lack of control, point strongly
to the need for further inner exploration—and a search
for a better means than presently available to attain some
sense of stability and resolution.

THERE ARE many other angles to the multifaceted surface
of a dream. Among the important reflections, these are
especially worth considering:

1. What is the overall picture of yourself that emerges in
the dream? What are your main concerns? How well or
poorly are you functioning? What are your ways of coping?
With what success?

2. It is important, too, to scan a dream for your pictures of
others. With whom are you concerned? Are these people a
source of threat or satisfaction? How do you interact with
them and they with you? What does the dream tell you about
the people it portrays? What does it tell you about your
general view of men, women, children, friends, relatives,
animals, property, et cetera?

3. What needs and desires are reflected in the dream? Note your satisfactions and frustrations. How do they come about? How are you dealing with them?

4. What appear to be your main conflicts and emotional problems? Manifest dreams are often sensitive to emotional issues, and sometimes portray aspects of emotionally charged situations directly. How well are you dealing with these conflicts? Are they being resolved or continuing unmodified?

5. What does the dream tell you about your sense of self, your self-esteem, and your self-image? Does the dream express sexual and aggressive needs? How are they being dealt with? Do you feel guilty in the dream? Approved of? Disapproved of? Are you proceeding openly and smoothly, or are you defensive and conscience-stricken?

6. What is the predominant mood of the dream? Is it positive or negative? Does it change in the course of the dream? If so, how?

7. Finally, to what extent do the images of the dream touch on past events, including those from childhood? Are past and present related in some way, and if so, how? What does this relationship say about the future? Are you attempting to handle a present situation as you handled a similar one in the past? Are you warning yourself not to make the same mistake twice?

There are, then, many facets to a manifest dream. Because of the enormous number of possibilities for analysis when working with the surface elements of a dream, it is important to adopt two contradictory attitudes—first one and then the other, in alternating sequence. On the one hand, focus on and develop the most powerful images in the manifest dream. Accept these as strong messages, and analyze them for your view of yourself and significant others. Take a look at the main characters, the overarching themes, the central setting, and the unfolding of the dream experience. Shape these into clear, strong, fresh insights to the extent that this is possible.

While you are doing this, from time to time take a closer look at the minor details of the dream. A dream will often portray through a coincidental image an important aspect of its major message. This is a defensive strategy that you need to defeat by paying attention to what seem to be unimportant elements in a dream.

For example, Adrienne had spent a great deal of time thinking about the dream setting as her apartment. But she had avoided recognizing that the specific location of the dream's action was her bedroom. When she focused on this seemingly minor element, she was led to recall that she had been to bed with a man other than Dennis the night before her apartment had been broken into. Adrienne had felt bad about this liaison, particularly since the man in question had been interested in little more than a one-night stand. Now she realized that she felt brutalized and demoralized by the encounter; in retrospect, she hated the man and wanted to fight off the memory and the feelings involved. Now the image of her boyfriend/father removing the man from her bedroom had an entirely different meaning. Attention to a seemingly minor detail opened up an extensive avenue of associations of great import to Adrienne.

This last illustration brings us to some of the limitations of the insights available to us through an examination of a manifest dream in isolation—no matter how meticulous. By focusing on the surface elements of a dream, we often miss important triggers for a dream experience. It is these triggers that have shaped the dream, and they also provide the dream with some of its most pertinent and surprising meanings.

As we have seen, a manifest dream is only half a dream.

As such, it only tells half a story, and the other half is lost. And that other half is rich and valuable. In Adrienne's dream, for example, she actually needed to free-associate to her bedroom to discover a concealed trigger for her dream, an unpleasant sexual liaison. To Adrienne, the intruder is both the unseen thief and the sexual partner— the first revealed on the surface of the dream, and the second revealed only through associations that undid the disguise involved.

On the manifest level, there is violence between Adrienne and the criminal intruder. Latently and disguised within the dream is an unconscious sense that the sexual encounter of the other night had been violent—experienced as a violation and evoking feelings of recrimination. Adrienne recalled her feeling of being suffocated by the man. And she realized how fervently she hoped that Dennis would rescue her from self-destructive relationships with men. In fact, now she remembered how her father had forbidden her to see a boy with whom she'd become involved as a freshman in high school—a reckless sort of kid who hung out with a street gang. Her father had said he was nothing but an underage criminal.

Examining a manifest dream tends to produce isolated and static images, difficult to shape into a meaningful whole. They can tell us only one of several stories embodied in the dream. The underlying stories, which have been disguised and transformed, are most pertinently related to our unresolved emotional concerns. And it is these encoded stories that emerge from an analysis of a dream that takes into account triggers, transformations, and disguised messages.

However rich and surprising the insights derived from a manifest dream, confining yourself to that aspect of the dream alone not only ensures the avoidance of critical emotional issues, but also leads to an impression of the dream as some type of imagination work—as an expression of wishes, fantasies, and fancy. Limiting yourself to the manifest dream will make it more difficult for you to recognize that dreams reflect incisive perceptions of others and are often deeply in touch with unnoticed realities concerning yourself and your life situations.

Finally, it is almost impossible to safeguard an impression drawn from a manifest dream content with some kind of validating or supportive realization. An extraction from the surface of the dream tends to be so simple and straightforward that we are likely to accept it at face value with little discrimination. And although we can check out these potential insights, we never get to the rich and more surprising network of associations that can provide validation by virtue of a sense of the unexpected.

Therefore, when you are in the process of extracting meaning from a manifest dream, allow these surface dream images to become points of departure for journeys into free association and into the unexpected.

9
THE MIDDLE LAYERS OF A DREAM

GEORGE, a man in his mid-thirties, dreamed that

he is standing with his friend Milton in front of an old, gray, shingled house. Milton gives George his wallet with two $50 bills in it.

On the surface of this dream is the pleasant image of receiving money from a friend. In the simplicity of the manifest images, George noted that there were only two characters in the dream—himself and Milton. In the context of this dream, George saw himself as a recipient, perhaps as needy. He saw Milton as someone generous and giving. The dream as dreamed, therefore, alerted George to two areas of possible concern: his friendship with Milton, and his concerns about money. George did have serious problems in both these areas. So the central themes of the manifest dream corresponded to major themes in his life.

George didn't entirely recognize the setting, but it suggested a house in which he had lived until he was seven years old. His present apartment was located in downtown Philadelphia in a brownstone building that had been painted gray. George's living quarters, a theme suggested by the setting, were also a major worry for him at this time. Synthesized, the manifest dream suggested that George was in need of money, that this need was connected to his apartment, and that his requirements were or would be met by a gift from Milton.

In waking life, George's apartment had been offered to him for purchase, and he didn't have enough money to negotiate the deal. The dream clearly centered on this, a major issue in his life and a major trigger for the dream. Simply knowing the dream stimulus and placing the dream in the flow of George's life, the dream begins to resonate with meaning—even on the surface. The dream is no longer a sequence of fragmented images, but has been converted into a rather moving story.

THE QUESTION is: How do we get beneath the surface of this—or any—dream? How can we analyze a dream to arrive at its unconscious, or hidden, contents? One basic problem here is that the term unconscious is used to describe dozens of different phenomena. What is the dreamer actually looking for? Freud used two different terms for material that is not immediately conscious—preconscious, to indicate mental contents that are beyond awareness but are readily accessible to consciousness; and unconscious, to indicate mental contents that are barred access to awareness and are in a state of repression. For our purposes, should we define unconscious as anything of which we are unaware at a given moment?

This is a conveniently broad definition, but it isn't really very helpful. Take George, for example. As he considers his dream, his first thought is Wow, I sure could use that

money. Is this thought unconscious, since he wasn't thinking it five minutes before? Although this is technically true,
the description does not help us to identify the images and
contents outside of awareness that are most relevant to
George's emotional problems—their unconscious contents as they relate to the origins of his difficulties, and his
inability to resolve them.

The idea that the unconscious realm contains everything beyond awareness at a particular moment would imply
that all you need do is to think of image after image when
analyzing a dream, and lo and behold, you'll have its unconscious meanings. But this approach is arbitrary and un-
wieldy. Everything that we think about after remembering
a dream is not necessarily meaningful or emotionally pertinent. In the course of free associating, George could
easily ruminate about a hundred situations related in some
way to receiving money—including the price of chopped
liver and wishing he would win the lottery and could eat
his way around the world. Does that mean that his dream
is *really* about delicatessens, gambling, and travel?

A common variation on this "anything goes" approach
to unconscious meaning is the "your guess is as good as
mine" theory, to which a surprising number of psycho-
therapists subscribe. One might expect that the dreamer's
guess would be given precedence in this particular approach, but the situation is often the reverse: The dreamer
will take a stranger's interpretation over his or her own,
especially if that stranger happens to be a "professional,"
or a self-proclaimed dream expert who is quick to see a
surface implication.

George had the thought that it would have been nice
if the $50 bills were actually $50,000 bills, leading him to
recognize his unconscious wish for huge amounts of money.

George's friend Marcos, however, told him that the dream was confronting him with his greed and his neediness. Sarah, George's girlfriend, told him the dream proved he was tight with money and takes more than he gives—a complaint she had had from time to time in their relationship. Steve, George's boss, who knows something about Freudian symbolism, told George that his wallet represented the womb, and that the dream symbolized George's secret wish to be a woman and to be impregnated by Milton.

What's happening here is that each would-be interpreter is using a different theory or idea about George to organize the dream images. This is really the only way to approach the middle layers of dream meaning without getting lost in the "infinite domain" concept of unconscious experience. But the ideas that George's friends are using to guide their interpretations are derived from their own experiences—not from George's self-experience. One can assume that each is drawing from unconscious perceptions of George in his relationship to them, so that their speculations may contain a grain of truth. But this element of truth is not emerging from the dream as such; the dream is being used as a vehicle for their own feelings and ideas.

I have said throughout this book that I believe a meaningful dream analysis requires that one know the waking-life trigger that set off the dream. The trigger situation organizes the images so that they can be seen as an emotional response pattern to a real situation. Knowing the trigger situation naturally and appropriately limits what we understand as unconscious content to a particular problem or set of problems.

There is also a more direct, context-free approach to the middle layers of a dream. Use this approach if you have no idea what has set off the dream images; it will often lead you to trigger situations, and it can give you a sense of the overall emotional issues being worked over in the unconscious system.

The middle layers of the dream contain all nonmanifest content in three types of "messages"—implications or inferences, symbols, and symbolic stories. There are, as a result, three major approaches to the unconscious contents that comprise the middle layers of a dream:

1. **Inference Making—Getting at Implications.** In examining a manifest dream, one can detect a wide range of implied messages and meanings. These can be extracted from the dream by pondering the dream images and inferring meaning. The dream is taken at face value and extended on its own terms (in contrast to trigger decoding, where a dream scene and its characters are always viewed as representing someone and something else). Implied meanings may also be discovered by free-associating to a dream and identifying the images, incidents, memories, and the like to which the dream is related.

This has been the level of interpretation that we have been discussing so far. The images in George's dream, for example, imply needing money, being open to accepting gifts, extending help, and so forth.

2. **Isolated Symbolic Decoding.** We come now to readings of dream meaning that are more complex than scanning the dream's manifest contents or recognizing evident or covert implications. A symbol is an image that stands for something else. If a particular image, perception, fantasy, or wish is of some threat, it is given a measure of disguise (actually displacement from the original item and then disguise) and portrayed in a dream by means of a substitute. We recognize and decode a dream symbol by reversing or undoing the mechanisms of displacment and disguise that created the image. As we have already discussed, a surface symbol bears

some resemblance to or connection with the underlying image that needed to be disguised.

Symbols are discovered through intuition, formal knowledge of symbols used by all people, and self-awareness of symbols of your own. George's boss, Steve, was attempting to decode the symbols in George's dream by telling him that his wallet represented a womb, and that receiving money from Milton was equivalent to becoming pregnant by Milton. This is the kind of symbolic imagery that Freud considered universal; he believed that any object that duplicated the shape or function of a bodily orifice would be used in a dream to symbolize desires or wishes concerning that part of the body. This is why certain symbols are intuitively obvious.

Dreams do make use of this symbolic level of meaning, but, again, outside of some specific context in waking life, interpretations like Steve's are of limited value. Key questions, such as Why now? and For what reason? remain unanswered. After all, what can George do with the idea that he's entertaining a secret wish to be impregnated by his friend Milton?

Once you are working with your dreams regularly, you will become aware of your own personal symbols; these are images that become suffused with meaning because of your associations over time, so that your dreams will use them as a kind of shorthand reference to complex emotional situations. For example, Chester, who had dreamed of being captured by kidnappers in his ex-girlfriend's farmhouse, might well have another dream that portrays that farmhouse. Because of his work with the original dream, he will know that the image of Celeste's farmhouse is his own symbol of feeling trapped and helplessly enraged. Chester may also dream again of failing to connect with someone by telephone, in which case he will recognize immediately that he has used a symbol for noncommunication. When you work with your dreams regularly, you will notice many personal symbols recurring and becoming more meaningful.

3. **Detection of Isolated Symbolic Narratives.** Symbols may

be imaginatively woven into sequences—stories made up of wishes, daydreams, fantasies, and memories. Because these stories are symbolically disguised and beyond the awareness of the dreamer, they are called unconscious fantasies. These unconscious fantasies are usually seen as products of the dreamer's imagination—at best, attempts to solve emotionally difficult situations with imagined strategies impossible in waking life. These fantasied images, though they may be seen as reactions to trigger situations, are most often formulated without a context or active stimulus. These responses are not seen to involve encoded perceptions of reality; instead, the stress here is on disguised daydreams that are thought to be disconnected from reality—inner products of the mind. They generate constructions that tend to correspond to the general tendencies of the dreamer rather than functioning as a specific fantasied response to an immediate emotional situation. But, when making this kind of surmise, it is best to connect the fantasy to a current trigger situation.

Chester, for example, may have used the house symbol to portray an unconscious fantasy of entrapment and endangerment. But this symbol could be extended and understood to reflect Chester's unconscious view of women in general. Chester might consider whether he unconsciously wishes to be trapped by a woman, and imagines the security of such an entrapment as ultimately destructive. His call to Donna could be seen as a wish for contact that is frustrated by an unconscious need to be rejected and abandoned.

Middle-layer formulations can also be made in terms of perceptions. People tend to understand images in terms of unconscious fantasies, products of the imagination, rather than in terms of unconscious perceptions—unconscious views of actualities. Understanding that something is dangerous in reality is more difficult than believing that the danger is imaginary and can be overcome by an act of the will. But many dream images actually reflect perceptions of something real—an experience, person, implied meaning—and so they are usually connected to triggers and therefore to the deepest layers of the latent dream. Middle-layer perceptions are perhaps best seen as formative way stations—a new reality whose specific cause or trigger has not as yet been identified.

LET US LOOK again at George's dream in terms of these three approaches to middle-layer meaning. As he considered the manifest content of his dream, George saw that the images *implied* neediness, his wish for a gift from a friend, a view of the friend as generous and giving, and a link between George's present living quarters and the house in which he lived until age seven. Some of these implications reflect unconscious perceptions and connections, in that they had eluded George's awareness before looking at his dream images. Some involve unconscious fantasies and wishes—such as wishing for huge sums of money.

The *symbolic* level of George's dream suggests additional unconscious meanings. Startled by Steve's assertion that the wallet symbolized the womb, George thought about the image from the standpoint of its abstract shape and function: A wallet is designed to contain something of value—but in terms of the dream image, neither the wallet nor the money in it was his; in fact, George was entirely dependent on someone else for both the container and its contents. That did sound as if it had to do with pregnancy and children. When he thought about the amount of money he was receiving, it occurred to him that $50 symbolized a midlife turning point. As he mulled that over in his mind, he began to realize that he had been irritated lately by Sarah's idea of going back to school to start a new career; now he realized that he had been assuming somehow that they would eventually marry and have children, but his financial situation had kept him from formulating any concrete plans in that direction. He was approaching forty, and Sarah was in her mid-thirties. The dream suggested, through its universal symbol, a far stronger wish for a child than George had realized—and the sense that he had no power at all to realize that wish on his own. He felt frustrated and angry about the whole business of working out a life around Sarah and her newfound ambitions.

The old, gray, shingled house was a *personal symbol* for George. It was while living in that house that George's father had suddenly been fired from his job. The consequences for the family were disastrous, because it took George's father some two years to find new and consistent employment. The family lost their house and moved into living quarters that were both inadequate and unpleasant. The old gray house symbolized good and happy times for George, and yet served as a reminder—a second symbol on a different level—of the disaster that befell his family while living there. Here George used a symbol to express a series of unconscious memories painful to contemplate directly.

At the time of the dream, George was concerned about an impending financial crisis. His job as a commercial artist had been threatened. There was every indication that he would not be fired, but George was depressed over the possibility, and he knew it. What he didn't know was how deeply he identified with his father's disaster. The symbol of the gray house in his dream enabled George to see that his hypersensitivity to his current job situation was the result of a strong unconscious fear of repeating his father's past experience in the present. And the family's loss of their house very clearly contributed to George's present fear of losing his apartment and actually moving downward in social status.

Notice that George's isolated symbolic decoding led him into a reading of his personal symbol in light of a trigger situation. This gave him access to unconscious meaning that was pertinent to an immediate adaptive context in waking life. When we are open to dream association and to a broad analytic and interpretive process, we are typically drawn to the instigators of our dreams—problems to which the dream images often propose solutions.

Middle-layer formulations tend to move rather easily toward deepest-layer ideas based on trigger-decoding disguised, unconscious perceptions. As we realize more fully that dreams are not imaginary products of the mind isolated from reality, but encoded reactions to real triggers, the less inclined we will be to draw context-free middle-layer implications from our dreams. At best, these formulations are a preliminary form of insight that must be completed through trigger decoding—into which it blends. A complete analysis and interpretation of a dream should move from the surface, to middle-layer conceptions, to trigger-decoded insights. It is for this reason that so many of the formulations discussed in this chapter eventually include some consideration of triggers and their ramifications.

George also connected his dream to the frustration he was feeling that he was financially unable to purchase his apartment. He had consciously experienced a number of wishes with regard to this situation—why couldn't his father have been wealthy? Why didn't he suddenly inherit money from some long-lost relative? Why wasn't Sarah rich or some sort of real estate wizard?

George had met Milton for lunch on the day of the dream. The two had grown up together in the relatively poor neighborhood to which George's family had been obliged to move. But Milton had invented a computer component and was now a wealthy man. George was certainly conscious of wishing that he had been successful like Milton. George had also consciously wished that Milton would simply give him the money for the apartment outright; after all, they were friends and the amount would hardly make a dent in Milton's bank account. It is easy to see that George's dream expressed this conscious wish in a rather modest way; this was the contribution of the conscious system to the surface of the dream.

In thinking about all this, however, George suddenly realized that the wallet in the dream looked like the wallet Sarah used. In light of his interpretation of the wallet as a symbol for his desire to have children, this seemed logical enough. Whenever he thought about marriage and children, he invariably came up against the same financial concerns that were keeping him from buying his apartment. How would he support a family? Sarah was a dental technician, her earnings were even less than his, and if they had children, she would need to quit work, or they would need to pay for child care. Even if she went back to school, her new career would hardly offset the money she would have to borrow for that education.

There was some logic in the idea that Milton's money could solve all of his current problems, but why was Milton giving him the money in Sarah's wallet? It was almost as though Milton were some kind of middleman, a conduit for money from Sarah. This, too, brought up a wish that George was familiar with—his wish that it was Sarah who had Milton's bank account. But now he saw that wish more crudely—as an unconscious fantasy that he could marry Milton's bank account, or more disturbingly, as an unconscious fantasy solution to his problems: If he were a woman, he could marry Milton and share in his wealth merely by having his children.

It took little work on George's part to take that interpretation a step further: George often felt more comfortable in Milton's company than he did in Sarah's. George hated the idea that his boss had come up with a stupid Freudian interpretation that actually hinted at something valid. But he immediately recalled that he had picked an unnecessary quarrel with Sarah on the morning after the dream, and he found himself feeling pressured by her expectations, even though they were not much different from his own. He saw a lifetime of financial struggles ahead of them and felt angry that Sarah took his role for granted as the one who would provide for and support them both. In fact, she was probably bringing up the idea of going back to school in hopes that he would offer to help her out financially. Which was exactly the tack he had taken with Milton with regard to the apartment situation. It did strike him as easier for a woman; if he were female, he could simply marry Milton, quit working, and get pregnant.

But this insight into his resentment of what he saw as Sarah's expectations of him seemed to be the tip of a more disconcerting realization. He remembered feeling uncomfortable with Milton when they were at lunch together, and he had deliberately checked an impulse to put his hand on Milton's forearm to underscore some conversational point he was making. He also recalled that on the same day he had quarreled with Sarah, he had gotten into an argument with a fellow artist at work. Now he saw the basis for Steve's oddly appropriate observation via his dream symbols. The artist George had quarreled with was homosexual, and George had provoked the argument for no apparent reason. By understanding the middle layers of his dream, George began to appreciate that his barely recognized envy of a woman's traditional social assumptions and capacity to have children had liberated unconscious fantasies of homosexuality. It was George's unconscious anxiety and sense of threat that motivated the fight with his fellow artist.

SUSAN dreamed that

> she's on a beach, holding on to a string. At the end of the string is the Venus de Milo, and Susan is trying to pull it to shore, but can't get it in. A man comes along and offers to help, but Susan doesn't trust him. He insists, and takes hold of the string. As he pulls the statue in, it strikes a rock jetty and falls to pieces. Susan feels enraged.

In terms of practical application, we now have the following steps to dream analysis:

1. Examine the manifest contents.

2. Look for the implications of the dream images.

3. Decode all available symbols.

4. Attempt a broader reading of symbolized fantasies, wishes, and the like.

In examining the dream's manifest contents, Susan noted the following characters: herself, a man, and a statue. It was clear to her that the man looked like Perry, a man she had been involved with for a number of years. Perry had a destructive streak and a tendency to be disloyal, but Susan loved him anyhow, and accepted that she couldn't entirely trust him.

By profession, Susan was an artist, a painter of large canvases. She had just had a recent, very successful showing of her work, and she was now attempting to take a new direction. But she had been blocked for several months, producing nothing that satisfied her. She wished she knew how to recover her creativity.

The characters and themes of Susan's manifest dream already suggested a wish to realize archetypal creative energy, along with her fear of damage—the sense that she had lost the means to express that energy materially. And the surface images clearly suggested that whatever she was after was ultimately shattered—apparently because of a man's involvement in her quest. In that sense, Susan realized, the dream had a regressive sequence: Her attempt to cope had been co-opted by someone else, and the outcome was utter destruction.

Susan's initial reading of the dream, then, was that it reflected her sense of artistic failure, but also conveyed a heretofore unrecognized (unconscious) feeling that her relationship with Perry was deteriorating.

The setting of the dream was a beach connected to a house in which Susan and Perry had lived together one summer early in their relationship. It had been a wonderful summer, loving and passionate, but, even then, Perry had a habit of disappearing from time to time, leaving Susan confused and uneasy.

On the manifest level, then, Susan's dream seemed to organize around her concerns about her creativity and her feelings about Perry. She hadn't realized how close she was to ending their relationship, and the dream gave her some sense of that.

152 DECODING YOUR DREAMS

We can see here that Susan's work with the manifest images has already led her to connect her dream to some of its triggers. What other implications can we discern from her dream/associational network?

Susan realized that her dream implied a losing struggle to get in touch with the creative part of herself, but allowing Perry to help seemed to portend disaster. In her actual life, Susan had begun to feel that her conflicts with Perry were in some way interfering with her artistic work. Perry's envy of her success, his demands on her time, the ease with which he created conflicts that preoccupied Susan—all this had had a detrimental effect on her painting. By strongly implying this destructiveness, Susan's dream lent support to these impressions. They led Susan to a serious conscious consideration of the negative side of her relationship with Perry, and to further thoughts about ending the relationship.

In this light, the dream image of walking on the beach implies both freedom and aloneness. Susan always experienced a great sense of exhilaration on such walks. The beach seemed to strike the most positive note in Susan's dream—her pleasure in being alone and her freedom to go where she liked.

As for *symbols*, Susan quickly understood that the Venus de Milo at once symbolized creativity, beauty, and damage. Susan deeply admired this particular piece of sculpture, and saw it as one of the crowning achievements in human artistic creativity. The statue symbolized on a personal level, then, the ultimate in artistic creativity.

The ocean is also a universal symbol for the womb. Susan's mother had taken a prescribed drug when she was pregnant with Susan. This drug, it had subsequently been discovered, caused damage to the reproductive systems of female children affected by it in embryo. Recently, Susan had been aware of midcycle bleeding, and she knew that she needed to see a gynecologist, but she was badly frightened that she would find out that she was never going to have children, or that she might need a hysterectomy—both realistic possibilities. Fishing the Venus de Milo out of the ocean suggests her wish for the perfect child, yet also symbolizes Susan's sense of physical damage; the image, in a sense, recapitulates her own fear of having been born damaged—unable to procreate.

The image of the Venus de Milo falling to pieces in the ocean as a man tries to reel her in symbolizes Susan's concerns on several different levels. Represented first is Susan's unconscious equation of internal damage and personal disintegration. The image also suggests her anguish over being further damaged by a hysterectomy. This idea is supported by the fact that her gynecologist is a man. Susan was neglecting to ask his help because she unconsciously anticipated his taking control of the situation and destroying her altogether. In that sense, she didn't trust him, so her image of him as Perry had some validity. The combination of symbols, read into the relationship with Perry, suggests Susan's feeling that she had already been damaged by Perry, and that their once beautiful relationship was about to fall apart. As we have already seen, these symbols also portray Susan's dread that her artistic creativity had reached its peak and had been destroyed.

Among the symbolic ways of decoding a dream, it is important to remember that every person and figure in a dream represents some aspect of the dreamer. At times, we resist carrying out this type of middle-layer decoding for all the characters in the scenario. We would prefer to think that a dream image of a seducer or a robber or an otherwise unsavory character refers to someone other than ourselves. But fantasies and unconscious perceptions are not restricted to others. We deftly, if unconsciously, perceive many unwanted traits of our own, perhaps even more so than in others. As we have seen, the purpose of a dream is to transform these perceptions so they may reach awareness in disguised form. What better way of dreaming about ourselves than by dreaming of others—especially if we are acknowledging a repugnant part of ourselves? And of course we will resist putting the displaced image in its rightful place as part of our self-image. Perhaps our only consolation lies in realizing that through condensation the image does apply to both the unsavory person and to ourselves. Once we shift from context-free fantasies to real but unconscious perceptions, we will have to maintain a kind of *conscious vigilance* to ensure that we clearly understand the implications of each character in a dream for our view of ourselves. Still, we may be reassured in the end that any hope of changing what is most unpleasant about ourselves lies in this kind of frank analysis.

It was easy for Susan to see how the Venus de Milo represented herself in many ways. But it was only with some effort that Susan was able to see how the man who shattered the statue also represented aspects of herself. By taking his role, so to speak, Susan tried to see the situation through his eyes. She found herself feeling the need to reel in the statue at any price, and realized that she sometimes pressed herself and others far too hard. As a result she often destroyed promising situations and relationships. Perhaps she was pressing too hard at the moment in attempting to realize a new phase of her work, forcing herself into experiments that would never work. The implied message of the dream, then, was that Susan should relax a little, not try so hard, wait for a turn in the tide, as it were, and allow her artistic creativity to return when it was ready to do so.

But dreams, as we know, are layered with meaning. Even the manifest contents of a dream contain multiple messages. So, too, do the middle layers. The man in Susan's dream also symbolized herself in her relationships with men. Susan tended to expect a great deal of a relationship and found it difficult to let things take their natural course over time; she pushed and pulled at Perry, trying to "reel him in," to possess him. Suddenly her thoughts about ending the relationship seemed premature; perhaps this course of action was forced and self-destructive. What if Perry were refusing to be pulled in closer simply as an act of self-defense against her insistence? Perhaps her attempts to force his hand were destroying the relationship. At the very least, she needed to think about this possibility.

The middle-layer interpretations of Susan's dream have already involved us in decoding symbolic messages in light of her associations. But we need to remember to focus on what seem to be minor elements in the manifest dream images as well. Susan thought about the string that she was using in the dream to pull the statue to shore. Much to her surprise, she remembered herself as a child, flying a kite on a beach, at the very moment that her father had come to tell her that Susan's sister had been born. In this light, her efforts to pull the statue in were related to yet another birth image, but this one conjured up old feelings of jealousy and anger, exacerbated now by her knowledge that her mother had not taken the same drug during pregnancy with her sister. The dream suggested strong wishes in Susan that her sister had been damaged instead of her, and perhaps fantasies that her sister had never been born at all.

All these associations made sense in light of Susan's

concerns about bleeding and needing to see a gynecologist. But there was more. Susan found that she was thinking about the phrase "being strung along." And she recalled with some irritation having been with Perry recently at a performance of a string quartet, where they ran into one of Perry's former girlfriends. There had been something peculiar about the conversation that ensued, something that had led Susan to suspect that Perry might be seeing this woman again.

Consciously, Susan had experienced jealousy, but she had also felt a sense of relief; she had been feeling guilty about wanting to end the relationship, and it made her feel less anxious to think that Perry was actively cheating on her and had someplace else to go. Unconsciously, however, Susan was experiencing a number of contradictory feelings: She wanted to get Perry "off her hands," but at the same time, she wished to destroy this other woman, to break her into pieces. And despite her conscious misgivings about ending things, she evidently had a fantasy of a violent "breakup" with Perry that would leave him shattered. She realized that she had recently begun to question Perry constantly about his whereabouts when they were not to-gether. In fact, she had been puzzled by feeling so jealous and suspicious at a time when she was thinking about leav-ing him. By decoding her dream, Susan actually found out more about the nature of her unconscious responses to Perry's behavior with this former girlfriend than she knew how to deal with. She decided she should "pull herself together" before she made any rash decisions about any-thing.

In general, a decoding of the middle layers of a dream should provide insight that is relevant to current feelings and otherwise inexplicable behaviors in waking life. There is, however, a tendency in working with this layer of dream interpretation to isolate the dream not only from its triggers, but also from the personal disturbances whose unconscious basis the dream interpretation might clarify. Manifest readings of dreams, and isolated efforts to arrive at middle-layer meanings, tend to lift the dream out of the ongoing, daily life of the dreamer. It is better to approach a dream from the outset with the assumption that it relates to what is going on in the dreamer's immediate waking life.

Nonetheless, when in a pinch, short of time, or unable to connect a dream to triggers and other life events, a quick and direct study of a dream, its implications, its symbols, and its evident disguised representations, can be quite revealing.

THE SURFACE and middle layers of a dream, properly deciphered and understood, tell us a good deal about a dreamer. But even this view of the dreamer is incomplete. Just what exactly is revealed by the middle layers of a dream?

It is important to understand that the middle layers of dreams arise because communications in the sleeping state are both symbolic and, as Freud described them, overdetermined. In the waking state, we ordinarily say what we mean and mean what we say. Our communications may have implications, but, in general, they have one meaning. When someone says "I just bought a new TV set," there are really very few ways to understand the sense of the words except in terms of their direct intent. In the dreaming state, conditions are different. We say what we mean, but we usually say it in terms of what we don't mean. And even what we don't mean has implications that we do mean.

This is why an image can contain so many meanings at the same time, which is what Freud meant by overdetermination. It can be confusing at first to analyze a dream, because the same image can be decoded to mean two completely contradictory reactions to the same waking-life situation. It is because of this layering of meanings—also called condensation—that there are so many approaches to unconscious dream content. Every figure in a dream stands for or represents itself—but may also stand for someone else in disguise, and always represents an aspect of the dreamer as well. Because all of these things have been condensed into one image, meanings can be intricate and multiple.

On the surface, but especially in the dream's middle layers, dreams reflect both our inner wishes, fantasies, and memories on the one hand, and our valid perceptions of others as well. The approaches to the middle layer of Susan's dream have emphasized those aspects of a dream that are products of the dreamer's imagination, secret desires, strivings, conflicts, and emotional defenses. In this overriding emphasis on the dreamer's inner world, we have to some extent neglected the role of others in precipitating the reactions that become dream images.

Our approach has been that dreams can be seen as a kind of internal drama. The drama itself is layered, in that the figures of the play, as written by the dreamer, stand on one level for themselves and on another for the dreamer alone. And the play itself is written out, as we have seen, on multiple levels, each with a current of meaning. This metaphor for dream formation is an attractive one and is held by many dream interpreters. But this approach holds the dreamer entirely accountable for the contents of the dream. This is not strictly true. Every reaction that a dream portrays is not merely a product of the dreamer's conflicts and desires; some are legitimate responses to other people's behavior that will tell us as much about those other people as about the dreamer's view of them. We need a more integrated approach to dream interpretation—one that takes the contribution of others into account.

Without this perspective, the accents of an interpretation will be skewed, the insights partial—and often misleading. And given the defenses that operate in the midst of a dream, much will be missed, typically the most important and best-defended unconscious meanings. Let us now turn to a more balanced form of dream interpretation that will take into account the totality of fantasy and reality.

10
TRIGGERS, DREAMERS, AND DREAMS

EMOTIONAL triggers are the instigators of dreams; that is, when the unconscious system registers a traumatic emotional situation and works it over, its efforts are often reflected in dreams. Dreams, then, reflect both the nature of the trauma as unconsciously perceived by the dreamer and the dreamer's internal reaction to that trauma. The raw and disturbing perceptions of the dreamer have been subjected to disguise and distortion and rendered more palatable to conscious awareness in the surface of the dream. Therefore, you can reach a full understanding of a dream only by undoing these mechanisms.

Thus far, you have been learning to arrive at the waking-life trigger of a dream indirectly—by working with the dream images in isolation and trying to recognize in them clear-cut references to waking-life circumstances. In this and the next chapter, you will learn how to come to terms with a dream by means of trigger decoding. This means unraveling the dream images from their disguises, guided by the configuration of meanings inherent in the trigger situation. In particular, this means noticing the validity of your perceptions as reflected in the dream images and taking into account the entire substance of your life and immediate concerns, not simply the dream specimen and its separate elements. To lead us toward a sound use of these principles, we will now consider in some detail the relationship between dreams and their triggers.

In the approach we are now developing, the dream is in some important senses not central at all—except as a valuable carrier of information otherwise inaccessible to us. At the heart of the matter stands not the dream, but the trigger situation—or what Freud called "day residue." One might suggest that if Freud had written *The Interpretation of Triggers* rather than *The Interpretation of Dreams*, our understanding of dreams would be far more advanced than it is today.

Life's issues are experiences—triggers, not dreams. Of course, we react to triggers selectively and in keeping with our inner needs and past experiences. And dreams do reflect both our emotional issues and our way of dealing with them, but it is the emotional trigger we must understand. Only then does the assessment and strategy reflected in a dream make full sense and serve us. Dreams inform us about what we are currently feeling, but knowing our triggers informs us about our dreams.

On a conscious level, we engage in many different kinds of struggles, but we also receive impressions outside of immediate awareness. These messages are communicated to the conscious system only in encoded form. The dream merely carries this information. Without knowledge of the battle itself—its participants, history, present issues, anticipated developments—the information being carried is intriguing but lacks context and meaning.

It is easy to forget that the dream is merely a message, an inner report that embodies a real experience and a series of reactions to that experience. And because the dream is the product of a human mind, it is all too easy to think of it as a piece of imagination disconnected from reality. Still, as this analogy shows, the dream is intimately connected with reality and contains an enormous amount of information about the real world. The dream is a reflection of waking-life issues—how we see them, what we are doing about them, what we anticipate, and what our future plans are. We need to be reminded again and again of the nature of a dream, so that in its decoding, we can better understand the emotional issues of our lives—and take advantage of the unique insights that dreams provide toward their solution.

IN TRIGGER decoding, we allow for the development of a dream/associational network and then unravel its meanings in light of the triggers that have provoked it. We undo the influence of the *transformation function*—displacement and disguise—and expose the painful, raw perceptions and reactive fantasies that constitute the most critical unconscious layer latent to the manifest dream. The revelations obtained in this fashion embody our deep unconscious perception of ourselves and others, and of the implications of the emotional situations that disturb our equilibrium. Reflected, too, is the wisdom of the deep unconscious system as it points to solutions to our problems that are unavailable to us consciously.

It is the strategy of the transformation function to disguise especially those situations which most disturb our emotional equanimity. As a result, particularly disturbing trigger situations rarely appear in manifest dreams in a direct way. In the course of unguided free associating, however, the mind is usually drawn to various conflict situations of one sort or another and to troubling events that occurred a day or two prior to the dream.

In exploring a dream, you should allow these allusions to emotionally charged events to come and go. And then, at those junctures when you shift from unencumbered free associating to scrutiny, analysis, and synthesis of the dream material, you can selectively identify the most compelling emotional problems to have surfaced among these recent events. Then spend some time looking for triggers that did *not* come to mind. Sometimes these are the most critical trigger situations in the formation of a dream and provide the key to decoding the dream images.

An emotionally charged experience that has engaged your conscious attention is generally not going to be encoded in a dream image. On the other hand, the most obvious trigger experiences may well contain *implications* the conscious system has overlooked or repressed and avoided. These are likely to be disguised and displaced in a dream image.

Not infrequently, a particular set of dream images and dream themes will point to and suggest an overlooked trigger. Monty dreamed that

a concert orchestra is playing music in the middle of a busy street intersection.

Monty was unable to think of a particular trigger for this dream. And his main association was a little obscure: He was reminded of a scene from the movie *The Sugarland Express*. In this movie, a couple kidnaps a police officer and demands that he drive them to the town where their child now lives, having been adopted by another family.

The object of this odyssey is the couple's idea of being reunited with their child. Toward the end of the film, they drive through a small town where they are treated like heroes, and Monty had found quite poignant the juxtaposition of this festive street scene with his sense that the two were already doomed.

Once thinking about this, however, Monty became aware of another set of associations involving a concert violinist he knew who had lost her job. She had been composing music and had dreams of becoming a great classical composer. She had been carrying out research at American Indian reservations in search of indigenous incantations and rhythms for a new choral work that had become a labor of love for her.

Monty scrutinized the *themes* of his dream/associational network as now constituted: an orchestra playing music, an individual being celebrated as a hero at the same time as inexorably moving to his or her doom, an ill-advised journey of the heart, loss of a job, dreams of greatness and of creating lasting work, doing research, being creative, being acknowledged for one's contributions. The themes pointed Monty immediately to a trigger situation.

Monty worked as a researcher for a pharmaceutical house. He had been working with a series of new drugs that he believed could lead to a cure for certain types of cancer. However, his excitement about the project had somehow touched off a series of disputes with the lab director, and he was beginning to think that he might be fired. Now that Monty thought about it, on the day prior to his dream, he had been talking to the director about a possible breakthrough experiment that could result in a new line of chemical compounds with anticancer potential. He had been so keyed up by the work that he hadn't paid much attention to the director's responses; when he played the conversation back in his mind, however, he realized that the director had seemed uncomfortable and had attempted to dampen Monty's enthusiasm. The implication was that Monty was a bit of a maverick and had attempted to bully the director into supporting an impulsive and perhaps misdirected line of action.

Now the association to the movie made some sense. The director might just as well have said, "Why are you trying to involve me in your personal odyssey? This isn't even your baby. Other people are taking care of such research. Leave it alone." Monty wondered whether the director in some way resented and envied him for his very tendency to envision a possibility and "jump into a car and go after it." Now he also remembered that the director had unexpectedly spent a good deal of their time together discussing his decision to fire another employee. It began to dawn on Monty that his dream was partly a response to the boss's displaced or encoded message that his own job was in danger. The conversation had been far more traumatic than Monty had realized consciously.

Notice here that the themes of Monty's dream/associational network pointed him to the trigger situation with which the dream was dealing. The trigger situation, in turn, led him back into the dream/associational network, where he could now decode specific elements in light of what he knew about their waking-life stimulus. The insights Monty gained by this back-and-forth analysis helped him explore and handle the waking-life trigger situation far more effectively than he might have done otherwise. For one thing, he took notice, with some discomfort, of the dream's suggestion that he enjoyed playing the misfit who would follow too large a dream to simultaneous social acknowledgment and self-destruction. This was an important insight that led him to temper his anger over his director's lack of support for his vision.

BECAUSE THEY are so disturbing, trigger situations tend to be quite elusive and difficult to bring into awareness. Once recognized, however, they seem surprisingly self-evident. Only experience will show you how persistently you may need to work with a dream/associational network before a trigger suddenly emerges. When it does, that situation acts like a magnet, bringing together the scattered elements of the dream. The synthesis itself makes the trigger seem so obvious that it is difficult to believe it could have been missed. It is this experience of having repressed something so obvious that gives one a sense of the power of psychological defenses and of the human need for self-protection.

THERE IS no dreamer without emotionally charged life experiences, and no dream without an emotionally charged stimulus. To place the dream in the stream of our lives, we must recognize three irreducible factors in its creation: trigger situations, the dreamer, and the total context and sequence of experiences involved in the interaction of the two.

At base, triggers are events that occur in waking reality—events that evoke responses in a person, both conscious and, especially, unconscious. They are constituted by stimuli that require us to respond and to adapt whether we want to or not. As such, a trigger can be positive or negative. Gratifying events, such as marriage, having children,

being promoted, and inheriting money, also require change
and adjustment. Sometimes circumstances are different from
what we expect or desire, forcing us to adapt. Clearly, every
dreamer experiences the world from the vantage point of
his or her own conscious and unconscious perceptive capacities. Therefore, every dreamer is sensitive or insensitive to a particular range of potential trigger situations,
and to certain dimensions or implications of a given trigger
situation.

What we have here is an interactive whole: Elements
of a trigger are selectively perceived and responded to by
the potential dreamer. A person may provoke a trigger
situation himself or herself and still not consciously recognize all the implications of that act, or a person may
inadvertently fall victim to unexpected and uncontrolled
traumatic events, such as an earthquake or a car accident.

When a person experiences a trigger, the sequence of
events is as follows: An event occurs whose meaning or
implications are emotionally charged for the potential
dreamer. In waking life, the dreamer responds to this event
in one of three ways: (1) The situation is noticed as disturbing and there is an immediate conscious response or
a decision to set the event aside to think about later; (2)
The situation reaches conscious awareness peripherally and
is given minimal emotional importance; or (3) The event
is not consciously noticed at all.

Whether responded to consciously or bypassed entirely, an emotionally charged event is generally worked
over extensively by the unconscious system. This may or
may not be accompanied by further conscious processing.
Then, when we are asleep the two processes come together, conscious and unconscious, under the domination
of the latter. In the unconscious realm, the ever-present

transformation function imposes a significant measure of disguise on the images being worked over. Still, the net result of these processes is a manifest dream experience.

Let us look more closely at this process. But instead of starting with a dream, we will look first at the relevant trigger situation to examine from the outset its relationship to the dream images it has evoked.

AT THE TIME of the incident I am about to describe, Peter was a married man in his late thirties with two teenage children, a son and a daughter. One night he came home from work and abruptly announced to his family that he had decided to end his marriage and leave. He packed two suitcases, and despite his family's efforts to dissuade him, he walked out.

This is very clearly an emotionally charged trigger for all concerned. It is a highly disturbing stimulus to which each member of the family, including Peter, must and will respond and adapt. Each member of the family will do so in terms of his or her own perceptions of what happened. Some aspects of the trigger situation will be conscious, and others will be processed entirely outside of awareness.

The conscious system is poorly equipped to deal with trigger situations. It appears to have been designed for matters of survival, such as acquiring food, shelter, and other forms of protection. This system will spare neither time nor resources to deal with emotional problems unless they appear to be life-threatening. As a result, the conscious system defends itself against awareness of trigger situations; if it cannot set them aside, it deals with them perfunctorily and disposes of them as quickly as possible. The irony is that in many situations we have no choice but to react at the immediate moment consciously and directly in terms of our conscious resources (unknowingly influenced by the deep unconscious system). This is why working with dreams through trigger decoding has adaptive value; it gives us a way to add a critical dimension and to tap the resources of the deep unconscious system.

There are two broad classes of meaning inherent in trigger situations: *universal* and *personal*. Certain trigger situations have essentially the same meanings for everyone, notwithstanding the personal attributes of an individual's conscious and unconscious systems. Peter's decision to leave his family, for example, will be experienced by each member of the family as a form of abandonment. But the detailed and specific meanings of abandonment and loss will vary. These variations will depend not only on the personal implications of Peter's behavior for each member, but also on the context of each one's present life situation and the nature of his or her relationship with Peter.

Similarly, the death of a loved one is universally experienced as a traumatic loss, the creation of a void, and by implication, a reminder of human helplessness. These universal attributes would, again, be common to almost anyone's experience of such an event, even a person whose ambivalence or antagonism toward the lost person might dictate an additional sense of satisfaction or relief.

Learning to recognize the universal meanings of emotionally charged triggers is an important part of knowing how to trigger-decode. When you remember a dream, or create a dream/associational network, and begin to identify trigger situations that could have prompted the dream, you should pause from time to time and directly analyze the nature and implications of an active trigger situation to which the dream may be a response. For example, an emotionally charged moment of intimacy universally involves closeness, kinship, and gratification, but also involves dangerous possibilities—potential abandonment, betrayal, and the like. In the presence of a trigger of that kind, we would expect our dreams to reflect some of these universal themes. Knowing these implied themes will help you to organize the dream elements and to understand better how the latent contents of the dream have been disguised.

To analyze the meanings and implications of triggers, begin by identifying those universal meanings that are self-evident. Then shift to the more personal implications to determine the likely accents of your own conscious and unconscious experience. The more precisely you can define the implications of a trigger experience, the more easily you can decode the resulting dream because the deep unconscious system processes the most compelling dimensions of a trigger situation, especially when they do not register in awareness. And, as we have seen, the deep unconscious system dominates the creation of a dream.

Usually, a trigger is most painful or difficult when it has personal meaning. Personal meaning depends largely on the specific context of the ongoing and past relationships with the individuals involved in the emotionally charged situation. Perhaps the most important aspect of the idiosyncratic or individual sensitivities in our reactions to trigger situations involves ways in which we consciously and unconsciously *select* particular aspects of a trigger situation to which we respond with great intensity on both the conscious and unconscious levels. Every emotionally charged situation has many conscious, implied, and encoded meanings. We don't respond to all of these. It doesn't matter whether a particular trauma has been imposed upon us or unconsciously orchestrated by our own unfortunate unconscious needs, our responses are quite individual. Much depends on intrapsychic (inner mental) and interpersonal (outward relatedness) factors. What are our areas of conflict? Our limitations? What issues promote sound mental functioning? In general, the greater our internal vulnerability, the more likely we are to be selectively sensitive to an aspect of a trigger situation.

RETURNING NOW to the situation with Peter, let us identify some of the most compelling universal meanings of his behavior. Apart from experiencing Peter's leaving as abandonment and loss, a family member might easily register his behavior as a self-serving unilateral decision, an attempt to render others helpless, insensitivity to others' needs, and a form of hostility—a willingness on some level to be hurtful to others.

We would expect, then, that each member of Peter's family would be especially sensitive to several of these universal implications of his behavior. If we were to compare their reactions, therefore, we might see a commonality of themes, yet there would be differences as well, especially insofar as wife and children experienced and needed Peter.

In addition, each would have a selective response that was idiosyncratically his or her own: Each family member would give particular meaning to Peter's behavior, and, once the conscious and unconscious meanings of Peter's action had registered and been established, each family member would react to these selected meanings in a personal fashion as well.

It is this entire sequence that would be reflected in a dream—the meanings of the trigger, both conscious and unconscious, and their transformed portrayal, along with the results of their inner working over in the unconscious system.

And of course the dream itself would be only one of a series of reactions to this particular incident. There would be conscious thoughts and feelings, evoked memories, behavior directed at Peter and displaced onto others, and perhaps even the development of an emotional symptom. And yet among all these responses, the encoded dream would have a special place. The dream would be the reaction that is most easily accessed and decoded for *unconscious* responses. Although feelings, symptoms, and behaviors are also encoded messages of a sort, they are difficult to decipher. And once deciphered, they do not present a concise picture of the individual's unconscious reactions to a trigger along with proposals for coping. Only a decoded dream will yield up this much.

FOR PETER's wife, the sense of abandonment and betrayal loomed large in her conscious thinking. By implication, she was convinced that her husband had become involved with another woman. She felt bereft and enraged, and was beset with thoughts of vengeance. For Peter's son, Scott, the sense of loss was paramount. However, Scott consciously saw his mother as a discontented, nagging woman, and he experienced a passing sense of admiration for his father; at least he'd stood up for himself. Peter's daughter, Amy, consciously felt a sense of emptiness and confusion; she believed that her father was probably going to live with another woman. All three felt depressed and guilty, as if each believed that he or she had personally driven Peter away.

These direct perceptions and thoughts led each family member to react consciously in his or her own way. Peter's wife, Barbara, cried long into the night after Peter left, and for many days thereafter. Then she became angry, and went to some lengths to discover whether Peter was involved with another woman. She began to develop headaches and to have vivid nightmares. Scott maintained a tough exterior and tried not to show any feelings. He immersed himself in schoolwork and sports. Amy spent much of her time talking to friends whose parents were divorced. In a myriad of ways, each member of Peter's family reacted to and worked over the trauma in direct and conscious fashion.

Powerful triggers almost always provoke remembered dreams. On the night of Peter's departure, Barbara dreamed

of a head-on automobile collision, with bloodied bodies strewn about.

Associating to the dream the following morning, she remembered in morbid detail the death of her father in an automobile accident. The gray color of one of the cars involved in her dream collision was the color of Peter's car. Without detailing Barbara's additional associations, the image of Peter's car immediately connected her dream to the traumatic trigger situation of the night before.

Analyzing the dream in light of this trigger enabled Barbara to realize several heretofore unconscious meanings of Peter's abandonment. She also derived some insight into her own reactions to the event, some of which involved feelings and responses beyond her awareness. She had had no thoughts at all in waking life that would have connected Peter's leaving to the death of her father, but the dream made clear that Barbara had experienced Peter's abandonment as the same kind of abrupt and violent assault that had taken her father from her. And she clearly saw it as final. And as a kind of death. Peter had taken something from her by violence and had in some way killed her. These were among the more powerful selective *unconscious* perceptions that Barbara experienced in response to Peter's announcement and behavior.

Another set of associations to this dream led Barbara to understand that she not only felt bloodied and damaged, in some sense violently destroyed, but also felt the need to do comparable violence to her husband—to damage him, to destroy him in retaliation. Although Barbara had consciously felt the need for vengeance, the raw and violent feelings evident in the dream had not been especially prominent in her waking-life reaction to the situation. Nonetheless, it was these raw and intense feelings that dominated her dream—and were creating her headaches.

Further associations to the dream led Barbara to remember violent fights between her mother and father, some of which had led to physical abuse. These experiences help to explain the nature of Barbara's unconscious selection of the unconscious meanings she automatically assigned to Peter's behavior. The dream also suggested that her own anger and violence toward her husband had helped create the crisis she was now experiencing.

For Barbara, then, her selected perceptions of Peter's behavior emphasized themes of death and violence, as did her unconscious reactions. Barbara did not realize this from the content of her manifest dream. Instead, she began with the trigger, proceeded with a reading of some selected and critical universal and personal implications of that trigger, and saw that they had been worked over unconsciously and transformed into a displaced and disguised dream of a bloody automobile accident. Knowing the trigger and knowing the universal attributes of its implications helped Barbara to get a picture of her unconscious responses to a terrible situation.

SCOTT, Peter's son, dreamed that same night that

> *a man is lying in bed, naked, save for an unzipped leather jacket. Lying beside him are two nude women. Off in the distance a baby can be heard crying, but the cries are ignored.*

Scott, too, associated to his dream. The jacket in the dream was not unlike the black jackets he and his father wore. One of the women reminded Scott of someone he had once seen in his father's company. He had run into them unexpectedly, and his father had been quite flustered but had led Scott to believe that the woman was a casual business acquaintance. Scott had detected an amused and proprietary look on the woman's face, and he had never been sure of his father's story.

The other woman in the dream resembled a classmate on whom Scott had developed a crush, though he had so far kept his feelings a secret. The crying baby reminded Scott of an incident that occurred when he was about six years old. He had awakened in the middle of the night crying, only to discover that his parents were not at home. Not knowing that they were at their next-door neighbor's house, Scott was convinced they were dead and cried hysterically for hours—even after their reappearance.

The trigger shapes both the dream and the associational

network. The latter reflects the dreamer's unconscious and encoded perceptions of the trigger, as well as his or her responses to it.

Using the trigger as our guide, then, we can see that Scott connected his father's leaving with another woman and with a sexual liaison—the man with two women in bed. His present experience of abandonment conjured up an earlier similar experience. It is significant, however, that the earlier memory involved the absence of both parents. This suggests feelings in Scott that his mother had abandoned him at this moment as well. The associations reflect Scott's past and present sense of panic, tears, chaos, and disaster; they may also suggest his mother's tendency, since his father's departure, to retreat into tears for days on end, leaving Scott to his own devices.

Through the leather jacket, the man in the dream is connected to Scott's father, but the same jacket also connects Scott to his father, suggesting both an unconscious allegiance between the two and Scott's unconscious identification with Peter's behavior. Despite a sense of abandonment and his evident outrage at his father's seemingly irresponsible and promiscuous behavior, Scott appears to harbor a secret wish to be like his father, and to join him in his illicit sexual activities. Scott's repugnance over these wishes had actually led him, on the day following the incident with his father, to ignore a show of interest from the girl with whom he'd been so infatuated.

Note here the typical contradictory set of responses of the deep unconscious system to a traumatic event. In the deep unconscious system we often experience several distinctive and compelling views on a traumatic trigger, which also contribute to surprisingly diverse behaviors in response to the trigger event. In Scott's situation, the dream/

associational network shows both hurt and repugnance on the one hand, and admiration and affiliation on the other.

PETER's daughter, Amy, dreamed that

a man in a black suit is flying away from a witch.

Amy realized that the suit was like one owned by her father. And despite herself, the witch somehow conjured up her mother. Amy's conscious feelings of hurt, pain, and the determination never to forgive her father for his behavior were contradicted by a far different view of her father's behavior in her encoded dream images.

On this unconscious level, Amy saw her father as escaping from a malevolent wife/mother. His escape was a feat of strength and a soaring that suggests Amy's feelings of sympathy and admiration for her father's decision. Although Amy consciously held her father fully responsible for what happened, unconsciously she adopted the diametrically opposite position in which her mother was held more accountable than her father. This type of opposition between conscious and unconscious perceptions, evaluations, and reactions is extremely common.

For days after her father left, Amy picked fights with her female teachers at school. Her unconscious battle with her father—and mother—was carried out on a displaced battlefield.

WE CAN SEE, then, that each dreamer brings his or her entire life history, resources, and liabilities to bear on the triggers that evoke the dream. Both emotional strengths and emotional deficits play a role in the automatic and unconscious selectivity with which a dreamer reacts to triggers and their meanings—manifest, implied, and encoded.

There are, then, three inextricably woven factors in the production of a dream, a unity that we may dissect into separate components and yet that in some ways defies separation and reveals its own distinctive properties. These are the trigger, the dreamer, and the dream, or stated differently, the traumatic situation (positive or negative), the silent or selective unconscious processing, and the transformed report. Using the dream and the dream/associational network, you can, with some work, get to know the trigger. Through trigger decoding, you can then derive extensive information about the dreamer, that is, about yourself and your deepest needs and desires.

II

TRIGGER DECODING

A DREAM IS a picture of the world—our inner world and the world about us. It is a personal recording of a multiplicity of images condensed into a remarkably small package—the manifest dream. The dream picture is, as we know, not a direct photograph; it is a processed image, a transformed image—a camouflaged picture. The manifest dream is probably the most complex and creative achievement of the human mind.

Trigger decoding is a way to take the manifest dream snapshot and turn it into a three-dimensional record of the actual emotionally charged event—and the unconscious responses it engendered. It is no small accomplishment to take what had looked like a two-dimensional picture of something unfamiliar, bring it fully to life, and recognize it as an important and valuable piece of yourself.

The heart of trigger decoding is to understand how a dream event is standing in for a waking-life event and to recognize all aspects of the relationship between the stand-in and the real situation. A dream is extraordinarily faithful to the emotional sense of the events it records; a stand-in image is not simply a disguise chosen arbitrarily, but generally depicts reactions and feelings concerning the real event that have not yet been consciously recognized.

The first step in trigger decoding is to identify the manifest *themes* of your dream/associational network. The object of this exercise is ultimately to relocate these themes in the context of the waking-life trigger situation. This maneuver—restoring the dream themes to their actual waking-life event—reveals the unconscious meanings of the trigger situation for the dreamer, and the reactions of the dreamer to those meanings.

LAURIE dreamed that

  a bridge is collapsing.

Clearly, the manifest dream theme is the collapse of a structure that one normally takes for granted. Something is disintegrating, falling apart. In a more abstract vein, a transition cannot be negotiated. One cannot pass over a dangerous situation. One must find another way.

After free-associating for a while, Laurie was able to identify two possible triggers for her dream. The first was her discovery on the day prior to the dream that she had a tiny, almost imperceptible lump in her left breast. The second was a disquieting confrontation she had had with her supervisor at work over some new dresses she had designed.

In terms of our analogy, Laurie's unconscious system took a snapshot of two different emotionally charged events whose implications had evoked the same unconscious response. Instead of depicting the actual events, however, the dream recorded the emotional sense of the events and located it thematically in a context materially related to neither. Once Laurie recognized the events that had prompted her dream, she was able to pry the dream themes apart from the manifest dream elements—the bridge, its collapse, open space—and locate them in the fresh context of each trigger situation.

Laurie then proceeded to analyze the trigger situations in terms of her identified dream themes. First, she connected her discovery of the lump in her breast to the image of a sturdy structure collapsing. When she put the two ideas together, she was able to conjecture that even though she didn't know yet whether the lump was malignant, she was unconsciously perceiving it as a sign of cancer, and experienced herself as having abruptly lost her physical integrity. She had never been seriously ill in the past, and her previously sturdy and solid view of herself had suddenly given way to a new image of herself disintegrating. Laurie had recognized that she was feeling anxious and concerned about the lump, but she hadn't realized that she was experiencing the discovery as a sign of total devastation.

A fresh association convinced Laurie that her dream was indeed a reaction to the lump she had detected. She recalled a movie that starred Brigitte (pronounced "Bridge-it") Bardot, whose breasts were repeatedly exposed in the film. Laurie had often fantasied having breasts as alluring as Brigitte's. The bridge symbol disguised Laurie's daydreams of attractive breasts, now imagined in danger of destruction.

Laurie now recalled an incident that occurred the previous morning, after she had discovered the nodule. Her fourteen-year-old daughter had come home from school with flu symptoms, and Laurie had become near-hysterical.

She wondered now whether her unconscious image of the state of her own body had influenced her exaggerated and unrealistic reaction to her daughter's minor illness. Indeed, an effective piece of trigger decoding can bring about meaningful insights that help to explain—and help us to alter—our most irrational and symptomatic feelings and behaviors.

One might wonder how the same themes could fit into a very different situation, such as the conflict Laurie was experiencing with her supervisor. In fact, Laurie had to work for a while to pull the dream themes out of the context she had been thinking about and examine them in terms of the problems she had at work. Perhaps the connection wasn't really there. But, actually, Laurie realized, she was resisting the connection, because she didn't want to remember that humiliating and unpleasant dispute with her supervisor. The supervisor had been dissatisfied with Laurie's designs and had had no interest at all in her ideas on how to rework them.

Laurie now realized that she had seen the supervisor's attitude as a withdrawal of support. She also felt that the relationship between herself and the supervisor had disintegrated, so there was no means of further negotiation. The designs she'd been working on represented a way of bridging the gap between her present position and a position in management, and the supervisor's attitude very certainly meant the collapse of Laurie's plans and hopes of achieving that end. Laurie also wondered if her job was now in jeopardy altogether; losing her position would mean the collapse of her professional support system, along with her means of financial support. Although Laurie had been concerned consciously with the supervisor's dissatisfaction with her work, she had been entirely unaware of her extreme response to her perceptions of this situation.

Relocated themes, therefore, are best thought of as perceptions of a trigger situation, many of which have not reached conscious awareness. On the other hand, as we have seen, these displaced themes also carry information about how you are reacting to those perceptions. For this reason, once you have examined the themes for a sense of how you have perceived a trigger situation, you need to look at them again to determine whether you are coping with that situation adequately or poorly. Often, when you analyze the themes in this way, the dream suggests solutions to the conflict or problem at hand that have not been evident through conscious deliberation.

In this instance, we can see again that two different incidents served to evoke considerable anxiety and depression in Laurie. She had worked over each of these trigger situations consciously, but much remained that had not reached awareness. These unconsciously registered implications were subjected to processing in the unconscious system; they were perceived and they evoked reactions. The unconscious system then reported out on these efforts. Because consciousness had already barred these implications from access to awareness, the unconscious system created a vehicle through which its efforts could find expression—Laurie's manifest dream. In doing this, the transformation function—the use of displacement and disguise—was imposed on the unconscious raw images and reactions. The disguise was not arbitrarily selected; it was entirely appropriate to the emotional sense of Laurie's unconscious perceptions and reactions. This is why decoding reveals so much about the efforts of the deep unconscious system to process disturbing information.

Notice, too, that the themes which served to connect Laurie's surface dream to its unconscious meanings were unconsciously selected to encompass perceptions and reactions to at least two triggers simultaneously. This is al-most invariably true of dream themes. Just as a character in a dream can stand for a number of real people at the same time, dream themes generally apply to several of our waking-life trigger situations. One might even say that no analysis of a dream is complete unless its manifest themes have been relocated into at least two or more trigger sit-uations. Remember the inevitable human tendency to ac-cept levels of dream analysis that aren't too threatening. Discovering one trigger and connecting it to the dream themes can easily become a way of ignoring more uncom-fortable waking-life contexts that involve the same themes.

CLEARLY, if we had simply considered Laurie's manifest dream, we would have had a sense that she was struggling with something disastrous. But we would not have known where to locate the disaster. Looking at a dream image in isolation is like looking at the image on a tarot card. It has general meanings of its own, it is evocative, and it can be used as a source of inspiration or meditation. But it has no immediate relationship to one's life. Laurie's bridge could mean anything—from the literal to the allegorical. Perhaps Laurie's brother is a structural engineer and warned her about using a particular bridge on her way to work in the morning. Maybe she'd just seen *The Bridge on the River Kwai*. Who knows? Since there were no human figures in her dream, we haven't a clue as to its emotionally charged source.

Given that every element of a dream in some way represents the dreamer, we could suggest that the bridge represented Laurie herself. We could even speculate that it represented some personal sense of collapse on Laurie's part. But all these impressions are floating in the air, as it were. They are so disconnected from the realities in Laurie's life that we have no sense of the issues involved. Even the notion that Laurie was entertaining a hostile or destructive unconscious fantasy would add little to our picture of Laurie at this moment in her life. We could suggest that she is not handling a conflict issue very constructively. But the dream might just as well be referring to a bridge that she'd be better off not to cross—an ill-considered divorce, for example. In which case, the collapse of that bridge could represent a determination on Laurie's part not to make an irrevocable mistake. Personal imagery does not always correspond to universal imagery. You really have to know the trigger situation in order to tap a dream's deepest layers.

By linking the dream to its triggers, the dream images become fully dimensional and alive. Understood in terms of each trigger, the dream takes on a specific meaning, and deals with a particular issue impinging on Laurie at the moment. Not only is the dream made more real and exciting, it now has practical pertinence to waking-life issues. The dream is not simply a product of Laurie's imagination, it is a sensitive, adaptive response to her life's issues. When we separate dreams from our everyday lives, we buy a measure of self-protection, but the price is very high. We lose the opportunity to benefit from an exquisitely sensitive and intelligent deep unconscious system whose contribution can actually alter the course of our lives—and usually very much to the better.

CASS DREAMED that

she is in bed, and her alarm clock goes off at the wrong time. She gets up, somewhat confused, and her mother ex-

plains that it happened because an angel was passing by. Cass is delighted with the explanation; it almost seems like she and her mother are sharing a joke.

On a manifest level, this dream seems puzzling and uninformative. The cast of characters, animate and inanimate, are Cass, her mother, her bed, her alarm clock, and, by reference, an angel. The manifest themes involve a mistake of some sort, waking up at the wrong time, ascribing a mechanical failure to a supernatural agency, and a friendly exchange with one's mother. These are difficult pieces to put together into an intelligible whole.

Without associations, the middle layers of the dream yield even less meaning. Clocks and angels have implications that can be said to be universal, but without a specific issue to attach them to, we can merely speculate. Is Cass concerned in some way with the passage of time? Is the angel a messenger of God? Perhaps a harbinger of death? All we can do is "read into" the dream; only Cass's personal associations can help us decode it.

Through a myriad of associations, Cass realized that she and her mother had been getting along very well recently. Her mother had always been an extraordinarily private woman, given to neither physical displays of affection nor personal revelation. But since Cass had broken up with her husband and moved closer to her hometown, she and her mother had been spending time together, and she was realizing that she had become her mother's main emotional resource. She wondered briefly if she in some way found that "alarming"; was this closeness happening at the wrong time in her life? This seemed too remote a source for the dream images. While thinking about this, Case thought about the weekend just past; her family had

taken her out for her thirty-seventh birthday. She remembered watching her mother interact with her brother's
daughters, and she wondered whether she herself would
ever have children. Abruptly, Cass realized that the clock
image in her dream was a reference to the idea of her
"biological clock" running down.

And a second trigger became immediately clear to her.
The night before the birthday dinner with her family, she
had gone to the same local restaurant with Wilson. Cass
had been deeply involved with Wilson some eighteen years
earlier when she was in her late teens; in fact, she had
gotten pregnant and they had been planning to marry.
Instead, because Cass was frightened of marrying so young,
she chose to have an abortion. Wilson had been badly hurt,
but saw her through the experience. Each had eventually
married someone else. Now, since her marriage had broken up, Wilson was attempting to come back into her life.
He was still married—"nominally," he said—and had two
teenage children.

On the night Wilson had taken her out for her birthday,
he had asked Cass if she ever planned to marry again. She
recalled that she had said something about having a problem with the idea but feeling that she probably ought to
marry before her biological clock ran out. Wilson had had
a strange reaction; he said that if it were simply a matter
of wanting children before it was too late, he would be
more than happy to father a child now and fully support
them both. Cass had not really responded to the offer, but
it struck her as ironic and outrageous and poignant all at
the same time.

When Cass had gone to the same restaurant with her
family on the following night, they had pushed a number
of tables together to accommodate their large party, but

she had realized at the time that her mother was sitting in the same chair that Wilson had occupied the night before. Now she understood why she had been so taken with her mother's interaction with her brother's children.

In terms of the trigger involving Wilson's offer, Cass could see that the idea of the alarm going off at the wrong time reflected her feelings of regret over the child never born; in a sense, she realized, she had been "alarmed" then, because the time had seemed wrong to her; she hadn't felt ready to "wake up" to the responsibilities of marriage and motherhood. And now, she did seem to be "waking up," but the time and context were wrong; in her mother's terms, the angel had already passed her by. In a more concrete way, the angel seemed to be the child that had passed both her and Wilson by at that earlier point in their lives. But the image itself pointed up a link that Cass had not been thinking much about between Wilson and her mother, in that her mother had a strong investment in the miraculous elements of Catholicism, and Wilson belonged to a mystical religious sect that believed in the agency of angels in human affairs. Both were likely to hide from unpleasant issues by concocting unrealistic fantasies.

Cass realized that her mother's dream explanation for the mistiming of her biological clock was actually a disguised version of Wilson's offer. She had felt good about his offer, and it had made her feel close to him, but it had also had the effect of magically "undoing" in fantasy a very real issue of biological mechanics; it also covered over a shared history that had never really been resolved between them. The rapprochement with her mother seemed to have the same qualities—it felt good, but none of the real issues between them were being resolved. In both situations, she was "waking up" at the wrong time, feeling confused, but hoping to avoid reality anyhow.

Through transformation and condensation, Cass had unconsciously created a manifest dream that spoke to all of these disturbing stimuli. Such is the pained unconscious poetry each of us is capable of creating, though we cannot know it unless we sensitively apply the trigger decoding process.

WE HAVE seen and experienced the essence of trigger decoding. Now we must flesh out the details of the steps to take to best utilize this method of dream interpretation.

Let's walk through a rather careful effort at trigger decoding carried out by Ellen, a woman of thirty, married to a man named David, and the mother of two children. Ellen awoke one morning and remembered having dreamed that

> she is at the site of a building where she had once owned an apartment. There is nothing there but rubble. The janitor hands her one or two items—a towel, a pillow-case, something like that—and tells her that this is all that is left. To the side, another building is standing with an overhang that extends over part of the rubble. Ellen feels angry and lost.

The longer the dream, the more there is to work with, the more extended the necessary analytic work to unravel its most compelling unconscious meanings, and the greater the likelihood of missing a link to a crucial trigger. Having a dream that is exceedingly long is more the product of wishes to shut off deep unconscious meaning than to know it. Lengthy dreams are so overloaded with triggers and potential unconscious meaning that they often prove resistant to trigger decoding. (Keep in mind, however, that truly disturbing triggers do not, like nomads, fold their tents and quietly disappear; they're more likely to stay around and set off a series of related dreams until they have been recognized and in some way resolved.) Since the length of a dream is not a matter of choice, you have to do the best you can with what is available.

Similarly, when faced with complex emotional situations, you may fail to remember your dream. You should then try to adopt the attitude that the mind encompasses an unconscious regulator, and that we can trust its wisdom. If this regulator intuits that you will be overwhelmed and unable to cope with disguised unconscious meanings at the moment, you simply will not recall your dreams. Or you may wind up with a kind of compromise between knowing and not-knowing by creating an extended dream that defies synthesis despite all free associating and analyzing. The point is that we do have unconscious intuition, and we can trust in our own unconscious judgment on such matters.

In this instance, of course, Ellen remembered her dream. Given its vividness, it was easy for her to fix it in her mind. This is the first step of any dream analysis.

Next, as you will recall, there is the job of completing the dream—of allowing it to be bathed in free associations. After sending her children off to school, Ellen had a few minutes free in which to associate to the dream. First she thought about the apartment she had once owned, and the fact that she had sublet it to an obnoxious woman named Jan. Jan had created so much trouble with the building maintenance people and with other tenants that Ellen was eventually forced by the tenants cooperative committee to sell the apartment so that Jan could be evicted. Although Ellen could have fought against the committee's pressure, it would have meant a legal battle, and Ellen did not have the energy to carry it off. Today, the apartment was worth at least ten times what Ellen had sold it for just five years ago. But for her, the apartment was in rubble; it no longer existed.

The janitor in the dream looked like a man who had come to Ellen's house after a small fire had done some damage. Gruff but sturdy, he had been in charge of the repairs, which went well.

The image of the vacant lot led Ellen in a rather different direction, to the neighborhood in which she had lived as a teenager. A long forgotten memory slid into Ellen's conscious mind, an image of her parents standing in front of a rubble-strewn lot, shouting at each other. In fact, Ellen recalled that not long afterward her father had abruptly walked out, and her parents had been separated for about a month. Finally, this line of thought led to some brief and vague ruminations about the problems Ellen was having in her own marriage, but by then she had to hurry out of the house, and her mind became preoccupied with other matters.

Later that evening, while David was out and the children were in bed, Ellen took some time to lie down and free-associate some more, actively engaging in trigger decoding and generating additional loose associations. She paused from time to time to contemplate the images coming to mind. Ellen made a special effort to identify recent trigger situations by looking at the themes of her dream/associational network. She then associated directly to the trigger situations she'd identified, allowing their meanings, implications, and connections to other memories and experiences to unfold. At other moments, she associated to specific dream elements.

When you are trigger decoding, the less you worry

about what it all means, the less you will be tempted to "read into" the dream or to engage in direct speculations. It is important to stay loose for some time, perhaps ten or twenty minutes, before trying to sort things out. The richer the dream/associational complex, the more likely you are to gain access to the disguised secrets of the dream.

After a while, you should pause and separate the triggers, setting them to one side. Then take all the remaining images—the manifest dream and your associations—as potential displaced and encoded reactions to the triggers. These latter elements of the dream/associational network are the source of the themes you are trying to identify as properly belonging to a trigger situation. You are attempting to lift a cluster of themes from a variety of surface images—the manifest story, associations, memories—and to interweave these displaced themes with the trigger situation that has actually evoked them.

You can now contemplate the trigger experience with an expanded awareness of your perceptions of it, particularly as they occurred unconsciously. Moreover, certain themes will clearly emerge as reactions to these unconscious perceptions. It is in these reactions that you will look for unconsciously derived solutions to problems the conscious mind cannot adequately handle.

You can supplement these efforts with occasional attempts to read off the implications of the manifest dream and to tap its middle layers of unconscious meaning—its symbols, fantasies, and the like. Finally, as new images emerge, or as you recognize fresh trigger situations, you will need to interrupt the process of analysis and synthesis to generate fresh associations.

Complex as this may seem, the substance of the effort simply involves free associating, identifying clusters of themes, transposing the themes from their manifest context to the context of a recognized trigger situation, and examining the results of these efforts. Basically, all you are doing is reversing a process that began with a trigger situation whose meanings required disguise. By the time a dream alerts you to the trigger, a transformation has occurred that needs to be undone.

As Ellen thought about the dream images again, she remembered a news story she had seen on television the day prior to the dream. A gas explosion had reduced three homes to rubble. Two women, who had been asleep at the time in one of the houses, had been killed.

A wave of emotion went over her as she pictured the unsuspecting women and the sudden, irrevocable destruction. Now she knew what the dream was about, but she didn't want to think about it. For some time now, David had been unfaithful to her, but she hadn't wanted to face it. Two days before her dream, Ellen had returned home unexpectedly from a Sunday business meeting to pick up a forgotten legal document. David was with another woman, obviously a lover, and Ellen had become hysterical. The scene had been horrible—the woman ran from the house, Ellen and David fought for hours, and, finally, Ellen locked herself in their bedroom to cry.

It was difficult for Ellen to think about that scene again. She was tired of thinking about what she was going to do. She had been sleeping alone, and would not talk to David at all. His shouted denials had gradually become pleas for forgiveness and promises of fidelity, but Ellen had been adamant. She wanted to leave the marriage, but over the past few days, she had been filled with doubts. Was reconciliation possible? Would David change? Should she throw him out? Leave with the children? Where would they go?

Feeling hurt, betrayed, angry, and depressed, Ellen had never been so devastated in her life. What was she to do? Tired questions without conscious answers.

Ellen went back to her dream. Lifting a dream theme and placing it in the context of the obvious trigger situation, she considered that her marriage had once seemed sturdy and solid but was now a shambles. It had been reduced to rubble. But at this point Ellen grew curious about the image of the building with the overhang. The structure reminded her of the nearby garage where David usually had his car serviced. The place was a kind of hangout for hoods and whores and other people who moved outside the cultural norms. Hoods and whores, she thought; this was clearly her image of David and his lover.

Ellen's thoughts began to drift elsewhere. She thought about a friend of hers whose husband had also been unfaithful. After a long struggle, this friend had decided to swallow her pride and hold onto her marriage if she could, but less than three months later, her husband came home one night, packed two small suitcases, and simply left. The suitcases somehow brought Ellen back to the dream image of the janitor handing her a towel and a pillowcase, saying, "That's all that is left." Little indeed, Ellen thought, again connecting the dream elements with her marriage to David.

What does it all mean? Ellen asked herself. She took a look at the manifest dream, considering the themes of decimation, rubble, loss, little being left. The janitor, the only other human figure in the dream, was a rough-and-tumble man who had been sexually involved with a number of the women in her building. The dream had depicted him giving Ellen very little. She remembered her reaction in the dream—the feelings of anger and of being lost. On the surface of the dream, then, Ellen saw only a sense of ruin and despair—little that was salvageable.

As she looked at the surface and symbolic layers of the dream in light of the main identified trigger, Ellen realized that she wished she could go back to the apartment in which she'd lived by herself until she had married David. But nothing existed there anymore; she couldn't go back. The janitor, as a stand-in for David, had little to give her. The dream reflected Ellen's sense of there being nothing to stay for and nowhere to go.

AGAIN, WE can see how limited the insights are when we stick to the manifest dream and a reading of its middle layers of unconscious meaning. Even when we take the trigger situation into account, the surface images of a dream will take us only so far. So Ellen went back to her dream/associational network and looked more closely at the themes the images suggested. As she connected them to the trigger situation, fresh insights began to emerge.

The gas explosion in which two women were killed was the first image to attract Ellen's conscious attention. Connecting the image to the experience with David, Ellen realized that unconsciously she felt totally destroyed by David's action. By lifting the theme of that association and placing it in the context of the trigger situation, she saw that the two women must in some way represent both her and David—along with David and the other woman. The image suggested that David's behavior had destroyed both Ellen and him, but it also suggested that Ellen was so angry that she wished David and his lover dead. Ellen felt a sense of closure in thinking that the explosion stood for her unexpected discovery, just as it stood for the lovers' reactions when she unexpectedly returned home.

This "explosion" was Ellen's unconscious reaction to the trigger situation, and as with most dream reactions, it offered Ellen a preliminary solution to her dilemma and indecisive paralysis: Kill the two of them. Hardly practical advice, one might say, but Ellen's recognition of the intensity of her feelings was an important insight. Knowing that her unconscious reaction had led to the wish to do the lovers violence, Ellen began to watch herself, so that she didn't do something utterly stupid in an attempt to get revenge.

Next, Ellen's thoughts turned to the building, the apartment she had owned, and to Jan. The central themes beyond that of total devastation include a troublemaker, a disturber of the peace, someone to be rid of, suffering a great loss, and the failure to stand up for one's rights (represented by her decision not to engage a lawyer and dispute the co-op committee's decision). Interweaving these themes with the trigger situation, Ellen was able to decode and read out several unconscious responses to the experience with David. There was, of course, a wish to be single again, in a sense, to go back in time—to undo the entire marriage by returning to the place where she had lived before she'd ever met David. The dream represented this as an unrealistic wish. There was also a view of David as a nuisance, someone who caused so many unnecessary problems that it was better to be rid of him—no matter what the cost.

Here the dream/associations presented a clear line of action: Proceed with the separation; you're better off without him, even at a price. This unconscious solution, unattained by Ellen in her waking deliberations, was further reinforced by other themes from this segment of her dream/ associational network. In the past, when Ellen had not stood up for her rights and sought out the services of an attorney, she had suffered enormously.

Although her conscious reaction was uncertain, Ellen's unconscious response seemed quite straightforward: Ellen should stand up for her rights and rid herself of the disturber of her peace. This particular line of thought, an unconsciously reasoned and adaptive solution, was also reinforced by her memory of a friend who had done otherwise to no avail. In the end, she was abandoned and left with virtually nothing—an outcome Ellen obviously wished to prevent.

Ellen next thought about the janitor and the repairman he resembled. The dream image was suggesting a second possible solution to her problem—reparation, accepting what was left and starting over. The deep unconscious system will often process two or more sets of impressions of a particular trigger situation and therefore offer two or more solutions as well. However, continuing free association and analysis will almost always indicate which set of perceptions/resolutions are dominant.

In this instance, Ellen again remembered the janitor's affairs and the scandal that had been created in the building when one of his liaisons was discovered. The woman involved had justified her involvement with him by citing her husband's many infidelities (notice the repetition of themes common to a dream), and then she had pulled herself together, found a job, and left her husband, the building, and the janitor for a new life of her own. Ellen had admired this woman greatly for her strength and resourcefulness.

Ellen could easily see that her momentary thoughts of reconciliation had given way to further images that pointed toward the advisability of separation and independence. In this connection, the image of the rubble took on a fresh associational meaning, namely, a dread in Ellen that she would not survive on her own with her two children and would end up poverty-stricken and bereft. With this image, Ellen began to realize that she saw herself as inadequate— she had not been able to maintain her husband's affections and loyalty. This was a painful self-image, yet one that could motivate Ellen to move toward a stronger position.

The associations she had to her parents' fighting and separating now brought more to mind. Ellen's mother had taken her father back, but her parents had never been happy together. For years, Ellen thought that they both would be better off separated—even if neither of them ever found anyone else. Going from the dream/associational images to her own trigger situation, Ellen saw she was warning herself not to repeat her mother's mistake. She also began to get in touch with ways in which the failure of her own marriage in some way replicated the situation in her childhood home. It might take her some time, but Ellen was now determined to discover the needs within herself that had led her to this repetition.

The garage, with its hoods and whores, brought to mind a recent drug bust. The police had pulled a surprise raid on the garage owner and one of his cronies, and they had turned up a huge cache of cocaine. The story had made the newspapers and caused quite a furor in the neighborhood. Ellen hadn't realized the extent of criminal activity occurring so close to home.

Relocating these dream/associational themes into the trigger situation, Ellen now saw her view of her husband as a criminal and addict. He was addicted to proving himself sexually with a constant series of women, and he was probably incurable. To stay with David would indicate an addiction of her own—the inability to survive without the marriage, or, in terms of another dream image, it would be like "hanging in there" for the sake of financial support. In that sense, staying with David would make her feel like a kind of whore. Here, too, Ellen's trigger decoding pointed to images of herself and David that she had not experienced consciously and to a resolution of the situation that she was not able to arrive at through conscious argument.

Tired now, and ready to fall asleep, Ellen was about to let her thoughts about the marriage rest. But as she began to let it all go, she suddenly remembered a telephone call that she had had from her sister Stacy on the day of the dream. Stacy had spoken with considerable innuendo about having been ill, about the stormy relationship with her present boyfriend, Floyd, about some menstrual problems, and a number of disjointed things. It suddenly dawned on Ellen that Stacy was indirectly telling her that she had gotten pregnant and had had either an abortion or a miscarriage. The dream image of the rubble now struck Ellen as connected to this idea of Stacy's abortion, as did the allusion to the towel and the pillowcase. She remembered a situation from her childhood, when she had seen a bloodstained towel and pillowcase in her mother's bedroom, and knew that her mother had had a miscarriage at home. One of the issues that had created problems in her parents' marriage had been her father's strong objections to having more children. Somehow, the idea of red flames gutting an apartment and the blood of a miscarriage seemed like kindred images.

Ellen realized that her dream was a combined or condensed reaction to two major triggers—the discovery of her husband with another woman and the veiled message from her sister that she had had an abortion. Oddly enough, one of these triggers had never reached direct awareness, only to be discovered in the midst of Ellen's analysis of the rubble dream. The two dead women most certainly on this level represented the two lost children. Ellen herself had had a miscarriage early in her marriage. She had felt guilty about it, because she had been rearranging heavy furniture before it happened. Perhaps she, too, felt like a criminal who deserved to be punished. Perhaps this feeling of guilt had kept her in her marriage to David long beyond reason, given his infidelity. Fair warning that she should be wary of her guilt in deciding on the best course of action in the current situation.

As Ellen fell asleep, she thought again about the towel and the pillowcase. In the context of the dream, they seemed trivial, even coincidental. Yet in the course of her dream analysis, they evidently represented the niggardly response of an unfaithful man whose wife was attempting reconciliation. Later still, they proved to be the embodiment (through condensation, and through displacement and disguise) of Ellen's memory of her mother's miscarriage. Ellen had not consciously thought about that incident in many years. She was intrigued by the way in which her dream brought forth this memory through such a seemingly irrelevant detail.

This is an excellent illustration of encoded recall. As we know, within the conscious system there are many memories we can recover directly, sometimes with a bit of strain. But there are as well a host of additional buried memories that are safeguarded by the transformation function and that will never pop into consciousness directly. Often, these buried memories from the past are the most powerful unconscious determinants of our behaviors in the present.

When you are attempting to trigger-decode, be on the alert for dream elements that evoke associations into the past, because these dream images may well lead you to otherwise unretrievable memories. Recollections of this sort will emerge only in the course of trigger decoding a dream, because their function on the surface of a dream is quite often, as we saw with Ellen's dream, trivial and of little consequence. Only when they are informed by themes from the dream/associational network and read in terms of trigger situations do they yield up the memories housed therein. Because of the unseen and unconscious power of these usually awful memories, it is especially rewarding to uncover them and come to terms with them consciously. Although the territory is rugged and filled with crevasses and chasms, the conquest of that space of the human mind that can be explored through trigger decoding is often its own reward.

12
ANALYZING YOUR DREAMS

A FULL USE of trigger decoding requires some time and effort. But there are many acutely troublesome situations where a briefer effort at trigger decoding is especially helpfull in bringing a much needed added dimension to the experience. An actual or anticipated crisis can often be better resolved if a short period of trigger decoding—or several such efforts in the course of a day—has been brought to bear on the problem.

Some people remember many dreams, some remember few or none at all. Another way of thinking about this is that some people are transformers and others are nontransformers. That is, every person is confronted with trigger situations each and every day and engages in both conscious and unconscious recognition and working over of the emotionally charged events with which he or she is faced. But transformers and nontransformers at this point diverge in their behaviors. The unconscious regulating system of the transformer permits and even fosters dream recall. In contrast, even though there are physical and biological signs that nontransformers dream, they seldom allow themselves to recall the dream images that reflect the workings of their deep unconscious systems. For this reason, the terms transformer and nontransformer are used loosely to refer, respectively, to individuals who allow their disguised messages to reach awareness and to those who either do not transform the inner workings of the deep unconscious system or simply refuse access to awareness of any transformed image that presses for expression.

The dreams of most nontransformers tend to be brief and very realistic; it may well be that their dream images stem from the unconscious memory-storage components of the conscious system itself. If this is the case, they are nontransformers in the true sense of the term. Nontransformers are less likely to use strong symbolic imagery in ordinary communication with others, and are somewhat more likely to experience emotionally founded physical symptoms. The mere remembering of dreams seems to relieve inner tensions, even if the dreams are not decoded. On the other hand, nontransformers will find other ways to cope constructively with these tensions. The inability to remember dreams is not unhealthy; it simply indicates a normal variation of regulating the communication of unconscious perceptions to the conscious mind.

Lab studies suggest that memory of dreams is also related to how soundly one sleeps; the lighter the sleeper, the more likely it is that he or she will awaken while dreaming and hence remember more dreams. People who sleep late in the morning have generally had all the deep sleep they need and during this extra sleep time are simply moving in and out of the dream state, so the memory of more dreams is likely.

Even though a dream is a derivative or encoded/disguised message, its very contact with raw, underlying unconscious meanings makes it a disturbing mental product.

We are all somewhat wary of these transformed messages, and as we have noted, we all have some defensive inclination to either avoid them entirely or to avoid submitting them to a decoding effort. This tendency is in keeping with the discovery that nontransformers—people who tend to remember few or no dreams—are often individuals who are for one reason or another overly vulnerable to disquieting messages, whether or not they've been encoded.

Those who have been severely traumatized in their lives are likely to be nontransformers. Death and loss, and their attendant anxieties, have visited them prematurely or with too severe a message—a sudden death or suicide of someone close to them, a near fatal personal illness, a major loss of any kind in early childhood, and the like. The unconscious responses to such overwhelming traumas are so painful and terrifying that these people prefer to ignore them rather than be brutally ravaged by the unconscious meanings connected to these incidents and to the latter-day triggers that rearouse their power.

But most of us have a varied dream life, remembering a brief dream one day, a long dream another, several dreams on still another morning, and perhaps no dreams at all for a period of weeks. During periods of crisis, you may remember very few dreams, in part because you are so occupied with the immediate needs of waking life. As time passes, dream recall is likely to increase, as all of the buried perceptions surrounding the crisis are worked over unconsciously. Then you should attempt to trigger-decode and analyze all available dream material. When under lesser stress, checking out occasional dreams in detail will help to maintain a sense of emotional equilibrium.

For the nontransformer who occasionally remembers a dream, brief trigger decoding is often all he or she can tolerate. At times, these individuals have moderate to long dreams, but the dreams prove difficult to expand through free association, and even more difficult to analyze productively. Despite this, brief forays into trigger decoding often turn out to be helpful in providing fresh slants on difficult situations.

If you happen to be a nontransformer and occasionally remember a dream fragment, don't become entangled in a fruitless maze of extended hollow associations and impoverished efforts at analysis. Try brief periods of trigger decoding instead, and if that proves helpful, then try a more extensive period of free associating and analyzing your fragment. Examine the freshness of the insights you are coming up with, and use that as a gauge of whether the additional effort is actually worthwhile.

BRIEF TRIGGER decoding is very helpful as an emergency measure when time is limited and motivation low, if you find yourself in a predicament, have suffered a setback, are experiencing a momentary emotional symptom—feeling anxious or depressed, or suffering from a headache, for example—or are faced with a suddenly discovered mental lapse. You quickly associate to and analyze the dream to discover at least one or more unconscious factors that have led to the difficulty. Whenever you are under emotionally charged pressure and have a moment to remember and quickly associate to a dream, brief trigger decoding can enable you to understand yourself, others, and the situation as viewed from your own deep unconscious system and sensitivities. And brief trigger decoding can often be extended into longer efforts at dream analysis as time permits.

AUSTIN, a young man in his mid-twenties, was in his doctor's office. He had been feeling ill for the past two weeks, and the doctor had just discovered some suspicious lymph nodes in his neck. Austin had felt them, too. The doctor recommended a series of laboratory tests and a biopsy, but Austin refused the procedures.

The doctor spoke at length, trying to give Austin some sense of the urgency of these tests, and as he went on, Austin suddenly remembered his dream of the night before:

> *A little bird lands on his arm and Austin is terrified of it, thinking it probably has some horrible disease that will destroy him.*

As Austin ran the dream through his mind, he recalled immediately that his father had died of some kind of peculiar tropical disease. He also thought about the fact that he had recently been sexually involved with a woman who had had some kind of vaginal discharge.

His mind drifted away from the doctor's words. Reflecting on his dream and his brief associations to it, Austin realized with a start that the trigger for the dream was the very situation he was now in—his visit to the doctor's office. This is an *anticipatory* trigger, one that provokes a dream in expectation of a particularly disturbing experience. Austin felt assured that the dream was connected to his visit to the doctor because of when he remembered it. (If the recall of a forgotten dream takes place in a particular setting, you can assume that the dream material is in some way related to what is going on at that moment, even if the situation was not anticipated in advance.)

Austin quickly picked up on the manifest dream themes:

bird, flight, disease, contagion, and death. Transposing these themes to the trigger situation helped Austin see that he was refusing the medical tests because of a morbid and irrational fear of discovery and death. As a teenager, he had often wondered if his father's mysterious disease was actually venereal in nature. This particular association enabled Austin to realize his fear that he, too, had a venereal disease, and that it would be discovered by the doctor. The issue was one of shame and guilt, feelings that were leading to an overly defensive refusal of medical procedures. With these insights in hand, Austin finally interrupted the doctor's monologue and agreed to submit to the recommended procedures. And though the doctor was clearly convinced of the power of his own rhetoric, Austin knew that brief trigger decoding had resolved the stalemate.

WHEN TIME is short, emotional pressure great, and a dream crops up, brief trigger decoding is the ideal analytic instrument. Although you may have to wait for a free moment, it is possible to do decoding even in the midst of a crisis. As we saw with Austin, if a dream pops in and you can make a few associations to some of its elements, an analysis and synthesis are possible—all in less than five minutes.

Whenever you find yourself in an emotional jam, feeling inappropriately anxious, or behaving in inexplicable ways, and simply can't find the roots of the problem through conscious deliberation, try conjuring up a fragment of a dream—or make use of any dream element that happens along. Associate to it briefly, then shift the themes from the dream/associational network to the recognized trigger situation. Again, the dream that comes to mind is generally related in some way to your crisis. Search for the triggers that actually provoked the dream, also, because the two incidents are often connected in some emotionally important way. Try to take into account your unconscious reactions to the earlier trigger situation and your unconscious reactions to the present one. Then take a look at the links between the two sets of reactions. Brief trigger decoding is a kind of emergency self-psychotherapy, and with practice, you can become a surprisingly adept practitioner. It can be quite useful when you wake up with some sort of emotional symptom and a manifest dream is available to you.

Brief trigger decoding is accomplished in one of two ways. In the first, you immediately recognize a major trigger for both the dream and the emotional situation you are currently experiencing. Since time is short, begin to transpose the manifest themes of the dream into the trigger situation. This will generate a fresh understanding of your unconscious perceptions and reactions to the trigger situation, thereby revealing the unconscious meanings of the dream as well. As time permits, you can then add some associations, examine the trigger situation directly for implications, and carry out a fresh transposition of themes into the trigger situation once you have extended the dream/associational network.

There is one major caution: At some point you'll need to reexamine the dream/associational images to see if they suggest an important but overlooked trigger. You should also think about the past day or two, in case you have forgotten about a trigger relevant to the dream meanings. As we have already seen, discovering this kind of emotional stimulus almost always gives a new reading to the dream/

associational network, in that the manifest images transpose amazingly well into a reading of the unconscious meaning of the freshly discovered emotional issue.

But suppose the tension is building, an emotional dilemma is unfolding, and you have a dream but cannot identify a clear prior trigger? Your first effort should be to take the dream itself and transpose its meanings into your disturbing situation. Next, engage in a brief period of free association, and then scrutinize the freshly created dream/associational images for the suggestion of missing trigger situations. The present dilemma may also suggest earlier triggers, though as we have also seen, anticipation of the disturbing situation may have served as the main trigger. If so, the dream/associational network will provide you with themes that readily transpose to the immediate trigger situation, revealing its unconscious meanings and ramifications. The point here is to allow for a period of free association, so that unexpected themes can be generated, which can point to an underlying trigger.

FOR EXAMPLE, Barry awoke one morning and remembered dreaming that

> he has been captured by some members of the Mafia. He is inside a house, in a room with two large glass windows, both of them bulletproof. Someone is trying to rescue him. There are two hoods guarding him. Barry notices that the door leading out of the house is open. Resigned, however, he decides not to try to escape.

At the time of this dream, Barry was a divorced man in his early forties. He was living with Vivian and they had begun to talk about marriage. By profession he was a computer software expert, but he was dissatisfied with his present job because the new president of his firm was difficult to work with.

Barry awoke from the dream with a slight headache. The dream itself was bothersome: Why would he dream of virtually surrendering himself to the Mafia? Was there some situation in his life where he was behaving in a way similar to the manifest dream scenario? What could be the trigger for this dream? Nothing urgent had occurred in his relationship with Vivian. His work situation had been chronically irritating but did not represent an actual crisis. Had he overlooked some disturbing incident? Puzzled, Barry began to free-associate.

The idea of the Mafia immediately brought to mind a newspaper story about a deceased mobster's son who had been convicted of racketeering. The son had appealed to the judge to delay the start of his sentence so he could write a book about his father. Barry had thought the request bizarre; in any case, the judge had turned it down.

The bulletproof windows brought to mind another newspaper story of a man who had held several people hostage in a jewelry store. The police had laid siege, and before the incident was over, two people had been killed—one by the perpetrator and the other by the police. The police had defended their actions in this situation by pointing out that the store had bulletproof windows and was an impenetrable fortress so they were at a loss as to how to rescue the hostages except by storming the place.

Barry paused for a moment to see where his associations were taking him. He could see no connection between his dream/associational network and either Vivian or the firm's new president. What had criminality to do with either situation? On the other hand, perhaps his un-conscious reading of his job situation and impending mar-riage involved a sense of being trapped, endangered, and in some way resigned to a life-threatening situation. Thoughts of this kind—feelings of being trapped—were certainly familiar to Barry. He had been working over these issues in his conscious mind.

Barry thought about the paradox of the police mur-dering someone they were trying to rescue. This theme failed to transpose readily to the two available trigger sit-uations, so Barry decided to associate a bit more.

He now thought about the open door in his dream: this led him to recall a film in which a prisoner was led to believe he could escape only to discover that he had been set up by his captors. They were going to justify killing him as an attempted escapee. Transposing these themes, Barry saw that he was unconsciously reacting to his own conscious thoughts of leaving Vivian and his job—he was telling himself that doing so could lead to disaster. Even so, there was no particular surprise in his connection be-tween these themes and those potential situations. The connection seemed apt, but uncharged.

At this point, Barry went back to a seemingly minor detail in his dream/associational network. The mobster's son had wanted his sentence postponed so he could write a book about his father. Startled, Barry thought, How could I have missed that? He himself was in the process of writing a popular book on software packages. He had been filling the pages with a host of new ideas that could have a major impact on both his readership and the in-dustry. He had been working with an agent and had been bothered by something in their recent exchanges, though he was unable to identify exactly what it concerned.

Immediately reviewing the themes of his dream/associational cluster—Mafia, racketeering, criminality, two hoods, being a victim of the police, being set up so one could be killed by one's captors—Barry suddenly realized he had been developing the impression that his agent was passing his ideas on to another computer program writer whom the agent had represented for the past several years. Now that Barry thought of it, he was able to put together a couple of disconnected comments that had come back to him through friends. These comments had hinted that this other writer was moving toward some of the ideas Barry had worked so hard to formulate. The manifest dream/associational themes transposed remarkably well into this trigger situation, revealing almost in an instant Barry's unconscious perceptions of the situation.

Notice again how extensively we can process a dimly noticed trigger situation in the deep unconscious system, and how much gets lost if the images are not subjected to trigger decoding. In his deep unconscious system, Barry was quite convinced that he was being set up and betrayed. And for some reason, he had not extricated himself from the situation with his agent though of course, with these new insights, he would certainly do so.

As Barry was about to put away this dream and its analysis so that he could get on with his day, it dawned on him that the dream was picking up on something else. In the course of preparing his book, Barry had used some material from one of his corporate files—material he suspected had been copyrighted by another member of his firm. Connecting the manifest dream images to this self-created trigger, Barry saw that he himself was the second hood, a potential prisoner of his own dishonesty. In his conscious system/thinking, his dishonesty had remained fuzzy, unclear. But in his deep unconscious system, outside of conscious awareness, there was a clear perception of criminality and plagiarism. The time had come to clean up that mess, lest Barry find a way of destroying himself professionally and winding up in jail. What began as a seemingly innocuous review of an only mildly disturbing dream had ended as a directive to handle two very serious personal situations.

WHETHER you use brief or extended trigger decoding/ dream analysis, you can't prejudge where your efforts will take you. A dream remembered is a dream worth analyzing. Even when your personal universe seems settled, dreams hold many surprises. And of course when you know you are under emotional pressures, the insights you can generate are often invaluable.

Barry's was a search for a missing trigger. Notice that he did identify two trigger situations in his life, but when he transposed his dream/associational themes into those situations, the themes didn't fit, and the insights he derived were neither surprising nor particularly useful. This is an important point. Trigger decoding is not an imaginative parlor game. Dream images are not empty vehicles that can be made to contain anything you care to toss in. Just the opposite is true. Dream images are jam-packed with real information about your perceptions of specific waking events. When you recognize the trigger or triggers that set off those images, you can unpack them in a way that will invariably surprise you or permit you to see a real situation in a new way.

In other words, when you decode a dream, you will always find out something significant about a real waking-life event—something you didn't consciously know before you analyzed the dream. If the insights you are deriving from trigger decoding are familiar to you or somewhat trite and obvious, don't assume that your dreams are handing you stale aphorisms; always assume a missing trigger situation. Allow yourself to build up additional associated images and your collection of coalescing themes will eventually lead you to the trigger situation that prompted the dream.

BERYL's situation was different from Barry's. The major trigger for her dream was clear to her as soon as she awoke in the morning and remembered what the dream was about. Divorced, with three children, she recalled dreaming that

> she's in a supermarket called Fair Value. Her niece, Nell, the daughter of her sister, Norma, is with her. Beryl begins to vomit and retch terribly, but she tries to hide it. She doesn't want Nell to see her or to sense her revulsion. As she turns away, she ends up vomiting onto some of the fruits and vegetables.

Beryl awoke feeling nauseated. She felt a strong need to analyze her dream and get some sense of the unconscious reasons for her nausea, but time was short because people were due to arrive shortly for an early morning meeting at her house.

The immediate trigger for the dream was a call the previous day from Norma. Norma had had a major quarrel with her husband, Wes, and she wanted to get out of her apartment for a few days. She wondered if it would be all right if she and Nell stayed with Beryl for a while—

just until she had enough time to think things through.

Beryl had experienced a passing twinge of annoyance, but she was quick to agree. She herself knew all too well about marital disputes—she had been divorced ten years earlier. Although she was tired of coming to her sister's rescue, Norma was family, after all, and if you wouldn't stand by your own family, how could you live with yourself?

With the trigger in mind, Beryl identified the dream themes so they could be transposed to the stimulus situation. Fair Value—what's fair and not fair? Vomiting, hiding it, not wanting her revulsion seen, messing up the fruits and vegetables—food. She didn't understand how Fair Value was connected with the situation. But once she had looked at the other images in terms of Norma's request, it was clear that she in some way felt imposed upon, poisoned, revolted, yet wanted to hide these feelings. The unconscious impulse seemed to involve spoiling food for others. Beryl wondered if she was feeling somehow revolted by Norma's request because it would mess up her life. Perhaps she wished to mess things up for Norma in return.

The Fair Value theme might be a reaction to those unconscious perceptions—expressing a cry to be treated more fairly. Beryl's unconscious reactions to her sister's request strongly suggested that she didn't want to comply at all, but felt the need to hide her feelings of revulsion. Consciously, these feelings were hinted at only dimly.

Time permitted a few associations. Fruits and vegetables, she thought, contain the nutrients we feed children, but something had spoiled their nourishment value. There had just been a piece in the newspaper about people who had suffered from food poisoning and were regurgitating.

At this point Beryl noticed that there were no men in

the dream. Men disappear, Beryl thought, and women are left to take care of their children. Beryl's own husband had disappeared with another woman. This is what had finally led to their divorce. This thought immediately prompted her realization that today was her wedding anniversary. Clearly, this was another trigger for the dream, but Beryl didn't know yet how it fit. She sensed, however, that the violent anger she still experienced toward her husband and about all that had happened in their marriage was powerfully reflected in the dream. For the moment, she set that second trigger aside and associated further to the dream images, knowing that she had to deal with the Norma situation later that morning.

Fair value, she thought. Men are often unfair, but, then, so are women. Like Norma, for instance. Norma was always dumping her problems onto Beryl, messing things up. Why should this situation be any different?

Beryl had a sudden image of herself as a small child, feeling terribly sick to her stomach but unable to vomit. If only she could have rid her system of the poison, she would have felt better. She realized how typical this was for her—never able to get rid of things that meant her no good, never able to spit out the poison, fight off the enemy. She just sat there and endured it and felt bad. Maybe the time had come to get it all out of her system—to stand up for herself, to get some fair value.

Beryl hardly needed to transpose these additional themes to see she unconsciously felt exploited by her sister, Norma—almost as though she'd been invaded by a parasite or poison that she was obliged to harbor, despite her own feelings. Norma had made her feel this way over and over again. She could see, too, the connection between her unconscious images of Norma and those of her former husband.

At this point, the doorbell rang, and Beryl was caught up in the concerns of the immediate external world. Her final thought as she went to open the front door was that there was no way she'd allow Norma and Nell to stay with her, despite her sympathy with their plight. Beryl had her own life to lead, her own children and lover, and her work to carry on. And anyhow, why didn't Norma and Nell stay in their apartment, and let Wes find a place to go?

Beryl felt that for once in her life she was going to stand strong and firm. Trigger decoding her dream had given her a sense of herself as able to withstand the unpleasant perceptions and images that evidently were part of her deep unconscious response to recent events. She had the sense that she was acting from a genuine position of strength and determination.

With this bit of trigger decoding/analysis accomplished, Beryl's nausea disappeared. Many emotional symptoms are based on the apt but disturbing processes taking place in the deep unconscious part of the mind. The symptoms speak on behalf of this system very much as dreams do, but their exact meanings are almost impossible to decode. We need a dream or some other narrative to get at their highly disguised messages. And if we do not express these unconscious meanings in some such symbolic form, and if we do not take the further step of trigger decoding the dream itself, this inner system of unconscious regulation will often continue to be channeled into physical or emotional symptoms. Such symptoms may pass quickly enough, but they also may recur; trigger decoding can generate conscious insights that lead to their resolution. Let us look more closely in the next chapter at dream analysis and symptom resolution.

13
DREAMS AND SYMPTOMS

DOWN THROUGH the ages, people have suspected that dreams and emotional symptoms—phobias, anxiety, depression, obsessions, problems in relating to others, psychologically founded physical ailments, and so forth—are in some way linked. Many ancient cultures practiced dream incubation rituals for healing purposes—attempting to cultivate dreams that would address the reasons for inexplicable behaviors or physical disorders and suggest solutions. In our own culture, it remained for Freud, in *The Interpretation of Dreams*, to argue convincingly that dreams and emotional symptoms are of similar structure. That is, both are largely the consequence of messages emanating from the deep unconscious system. Both are disguised forms of unconscious communication. As we have already discussed briefly, symptoms tend to be crude forms of expression and are difficult to decode, whereas dreams are articulated in narratives and images, a form of expression that lends itself more readily to trigger decoding.

In the real world, an emotional symptom or dysfunction is an inappropriate or maladaptive reaction to a trigger situation. We feel fear when there is no need for it—in an elevator, crossing a bridge—or we are anxious for no logical reason. But the roots of emotional symptoms lie in the deep unconscious mind, which has a logic all its own. To give a simplistic example, an individual may have developed a fear of heights unconsciously after a surgical procedure on an elevated operating table. The height has become linked to a fear of death, which becomes transformed into what seems to be a logical fear of falling to one's death. Free association might help to decode this transformed trigger, but as a rule, the unconscious meanings of a symptom are difficult to discern even through the process of free association.

Usually there are strong defenses against the revelation of the underlying meanings of a symptom. But the trigger analysis of a dream, or several dreams, often affords some genuine insight into the underlying meanings of a symptomatic disturbance.

Both dreams and symptoms have manifest content. Both can evoke a sequence of associations. Both are aroused by trigger situations, and when they occur in the same general time period, they each tend to express unconscious reactions to the same emotionally charged stimulus.

It was Freud who suggested that a symptom develops as a response to an emotionally charged stimulus, unconsciously perceived as dangerous. This sequence of events normally precipitates a signal of anxiety, and this anxiety mobilizes mental defenses. If the defenses are inadequate or fail, a symptom will develop, whose purpose is both to express and to contain the anxiety without having to admit the trigger situation into consciousness.

We can describe the formation of a dream in the same general terms. A dream is a response to an emotionally charged stimulus, unconsciously perceived as dangerous.

This sequence of events precipitates feelings of some sort—anxiety, rage, or whatever—mobilizing protective psychological measures. These defenses operate communicatively by calling forth the use of displacement and disguise. If these transformative defenses are successful, we dream an undisturbing dream. If they are inadequate, a nightmare or some other disturbing dream experience will take place. Or perhaps a symptom will occur.

We can see, then, that in general both dreams and symptoms are adaptive responses to disturbing trigger situations. Whereas an emotional symptom signals a failure in coping, a dream need not carry the same implication. In this light, we might ask, when do we dream and when do we produce symptoms? Let us look more closely at the interaction between dreams and symptoms and see how trigger decoding can teach us something about the unconscious structure of a symptom and how it may be resolved.

IN SEVERAL of the dream experiences discussed in this book, I have pointed out a connection between the dream and a particular emotional symptom. In most instances, the unconscious meanings of the dream illuminated the unconscious meanings of the symptom. Many of the dreams made clear that a direct and conscious understanding of the encoded perceptions and fantasies on which a symptom was based enabled a suffering individual to understand the conflict and emotional dilemma that had led to the creation of the symptom in the first place. With previously hidden issues out in the open, the individual can work over the problem consciously and find some kind of resolution. Indeed, an emotional symptom is a disguised substitute for conscious, emotional debate. When a problem or a trigger is pushed out of awareness, relegating it to the deep unconscious system, symptoms frequently appear.

In the last chapter, Beryl was suffering from nausea, an emotionally founded, psychosomatic symptom. The trigger decoding of her dream revealed an unconscious perception of her sister's request as toxic and unhealthy, repugnant to the core. Beryl connected these meanings to her wedding anniversary as well, and to comparable unconscious perceptions of her former husband.

We can see, then, that the unconscious meaning of Beryl's nausea was based on an unconscious perception that she was being poisoned by her sister just as she had been poisoned by her husband in the past—and in all likelihood, by her parents in her early childhood (recall her early memory of nausea and trying to vomit as a child).

Given this piece of understanding, Beryl was able to work over her conflicted perceptions and reactions to both her sister and her ex-husband. She resolved to refuse her sister's request and was attempting to come to terms with her remaining feelings about her former husband's behavior. Thus, the nausea that had been expressing these impulses and perceptions was no longer necessary. Indeed, once she had trigger-decoded and analyzed her dream, Beryl's symptom disappeared.

AT THE TIME of the following dream, Mario was a young man in his twenties, recently married. One night, as he was watching television, he had a sudden anxiety attack. Soon after, he developed a violent headache. Casting about for a trigger for these symptoms, he dimly recalled that the program he'd been watching had involved a story about a married couple who were physically brutalizing each other. This made Mario wonder whether his symptoms had something to do with a violent, but nonphysical, quarrel he had had two nights earlier with his wife, Monica. Despite his seeing a connection between that trigger and his symptoms, both his sense of anxiety and his headache were undiminished.

This is not surprising. The mere conscious recognition of a trigger without an associational network and a means of detecting its unconscious ramifications produces neither genuine insight nor symptom relief. His realization that he still felt violently angry with his wife, and that the anger might have something to do with his violent headache, is merely a cliché. It carries meaning without impact or surprise. Just as a dream meaning must be surprising and fresh to generate real insight, conscious recognition of a trigger for a symptom is not enough to alter the symptomatic state.

That night, Mario awoke from what to him seemed a nightmarish dream. He dreamed that

he has a sword in his hand. With a single stroke, he cuts a melon in half.

Still suffering from his headache and frightened when he awoke the next morning, Mario was able to calm himself and to engage in an effort at brief dream analysis. Monica had bought a melon for dinner on the evening of the argument, and Mario had cut a piece for each of them. But the tension between them was high, and the expensive melon served as the fuse for an explosive fight over money. Mario saw Monica as an irresponsible spendthrift; Monica saw Mario as controlling and unfair. For some reason, the fight had quickly escalated into a screaming match, with both of them calling each other names and barely realizing what they were saying.

Mario realized that the sword came from a newspaper story about a man who had recently murdered two people with a Japanese weapon of some sort. Monica worked for an importer/exporter who had extensive dealings in the Orient. Soon after they had married, Mario and Monica began having problems; Monica had turned to her boss for comfort and wound up stopping just short of sexual involvement with him. Guilt-ridden, she had confessed her near affair to Mario, and nothing more had come of the situation. Since her job paid well, and she could find nothing comparable elsewhere, she remained at the same company but made it clear to her boss that she had made a mistake and wanted to reestablish the professional boundaries of their relationship. At the time, Mario had been angry and hurt, but eventually the sharpness of those feelings had passed. When he recalled the incident now, he found himself thinking about a story he'd read about a man who murdered his wife with a knife because he'd discovered her in bed with someone else. This particular association brought Mario back to his manifest dream.

Mario sensed a chance now to make sense of things and to trigger-decode his dream. Two thoughts came to mind with respect to the melon. Since Monica had purchased it, perhaps it represented her in some way. He immediately recoiled from this idea, because the dream depicted him cutting the melon with a sword. He thought suddenly of decapitation. Then he remembered that as a boy his friends had teased him about his light blond hair, calling him melonhead.

Transposing the dream/associational themes to the trigger situation—the violent argument with Monica—

Mario realized that he unconsciously perceived his wife as having done physical violence to him; in principle, he had invoked wishes to do her violence as well. His associations told him that the argument had opened old wounds and generated enormous amounts of unresolved rage. Mario began to suspect that his anxiety was a response to his unconscious perception of murderous impulses in both himself and his wife. Clearly, the quarrel, although upsetting and demoralizing, was not important enough on the surface to cause an anxiety attack. And yet, Mario's panic makes a great deal of sense in light of the dream images, which indicated the ways in which Mario had experienced the fight in his deep unconscious system. Even his associations to a sword coming down on a melon/head suggest an action of violence commensurate with his violent headache.

As both his anxiety and headache began to diminish, Mario recalled that on the afternoon of the argument Monica had recommended a magazine article to him as interesting; it turned out to be about a wife who had been acquitted of murdering her husband because she was able to prove that he had beaten and brutalized her. Mario had made a feeble joke about a day to come when husbands would be acquitted of murdering their wives on comparable grounds.

This exchange between Mario and Monica is like an exchange of manifest dreams. Each version of the story is loaded with disguised, unconscious meaning—suggesting that each is not only expressing violent wishes toward the other but also feeling justified in those wishes by the other's abusive behavior. The deep unconscious system is especially sensitive to the unconscious meanings of such messages, which are almost entirely overlooked by the conscious system—by our waking awareness.

Until the recovery of this memory, Mario had no idea of the unconscious impulses and information he had exchanged with his wife. But now that it was all out in the open, he could see the exaggeration of his response, the perception of his wife's violence toward him, and the extremes to which their unconscious feelings had taken them. He also began to realize that there was an underlying source of tension between them. He and Monica had been struggling with the question of whether to start a family. They were both deeply conflicted about this issue, in part because they were still very much in debt. Mario had been attempting to find ways around their financial situation; he wanted to have children right away. But no matter what economic strategy he came up with, Monica not only refused to consider having children but also seemed to be undermining his efforts toward solvency. It was this underlying climate that had helped to make the argument over money such a violent exchange.

As Mario began to work all this over consciously, both his anxiety and his headache disappeared. Through trigger-decoding his dream, he had become consciously aware of the unconscious meanings of his symptom. Earlier, Mario had been unable to bear these perceptions and responsive impulses in his conscious thoughts and feelings. Thus his dreams on the night of the argument itself had seemed fragmented and he couldn't recall them. As a result, Mario had developed a symptom as a way of expressing the entire constellation of his unconscious experience. The remembered dream and his analysis of the dream had shifted these deep unconscious workings and images into the conscious system. With this accomplished, his symptom became superfluous. With the channel to awareness open, the channel to somatic expression was no longer needed.

WE CREATE symptoms when we lack some other avenue, such as dreams, for the expression of the disturbing experiences that well up in our deep unconscious systems. There are times when simply being able to remember a dream can preclude symptom formation. At other times, dreaming is not enough; trigger decoding is essential. Still, in periods of emotional stress, neither dreaming nor symptom formation will take place because our defenses are sufficiently adequate to shut off all forms of expression of deep emotional conflict and deep unconscious processing without symptomatic discharge.

Mario's dream was close to a nightmare. Having an actual nightmare is an instance when dreams and symptoms are one and the same—the dream is the symptom.

People who have frequent nightmares may be somewhat fragile emotionally. Almost anyone can have an occasional nightmare. In most cases, terrifying dreams from which we awaken are caused by severe physical illness or overwhelmingly disturbing trigger experiences.

When we have gone through a major trauma, we automatically process the conscious and unconscious mental (and at times, physical) damage. We then choose either to remember no dream at all or to have a nightmare—this is a matter of mental economy and expression beyond our conscious control. If we do have a nightmare, it is well to analyze the images that have broken into consciousness. If they are too terrible, brief trigger decoding will often suffice—at first. If, however, as with Mario, you begin to stabilize emotionally rather quickly, a more extended analysis is salutary.

Nightmares are disturbances in the guardian function—the safety valve role—of dreams. They are a dream form of an anxiety attack. Yet they are also a carrier of both the trigger that has set us off and, at least in part, its resolution. Decoding and coming to terms with the dream images and trigger-decoding their disguised ramifications is one of the best ways of insulating yourself against more nightmare experiences.

KEEPING IN touch with your dreams and carrying out a bit of trigger decoding each day can offer great protection against symptom formation. Of course, the situation is more complex and difficult in the presence of long-standing symptoms and chronic interpersonal difficulties. Under these circumstances, one has to take a long-term, quasi-therapeutic approach. With the symptom in mind, one must engage in repeated efforts at trigger decoding and allow a series of insights to develop gradually, much as one pieces together the segments of a puzzle. It is important to realize that, as Freud stated, dreams are the "royal road to the unconscious" and the best means available to us for the insightful resolution of the emotional symptoms from which we suffer.

14
DREAMING AND BECOMING

DREAMS simultaneously straddle (1) the conscious and deep unconscious systems; (2) three distinct but interrelated layers of meaning; and (3) the past, present, and future. We have discussed quite a few dreams that were prompted by the past day's traumas and that conjured up old memories, both traumatic and gratifying. At the same time, these dreams embodied responses that pointed to the following day's solutions—and beyond.

We evolve and grow, each at our own pace. From the dark roil of personal sorrows and rage and from the finer victories of soma and spirit, we move toward newer levels of maturity and more streamlined, more flexible modes of coping and surviving. And we carry all this forward, only dimly aware of the inevitability of that sudden moment when the entire system collapses, when death is upon us.

Psychoanalytic thought has at its heart the paradox of all natural life—that beauty has its portion in unspeakable horrors. Our finest moments of creativity have their roots in the deep unconscious system, its grim urges fashioned into art, poetry, music, philosophy by virtue of our conscious and available capacities. Gaining access to the underlying meanings of our dreams is a powerful means of enhancing our own personal creative capacities and efforts. It is as if we enter a realm where poetry is the language and prose all but left behind. If we spend any productive time in this realm, we cannot help but be influenced by its unique and analogical modes of expression, by its capacity for lateral thinking, by its special points of view, and especially by its constant generation of unexpected and creative solutions to our emotional conflicts and other problems.

The deep unconscious system embraces its own paradox; its influence on our behavior is very strong and far-reaching yet it remains completely inaccessible to our direct and immediate experience, unavailable as a resource for everyday coping.

This is why trigger decoding is so important. Properly used, it draws from a great well of untapped resources information and strategies for adaptation and survival. It is a testimony to our dread of the unconscious meanings accompanying these powerful insights that we continue to discover, lose sight of, and rediscover the importance of decoding our dreams.

Dreams belong to the domain of creative solutions— in art and in everyday coping. Trigger decoding itself is a creative activity that makes one aware of the rich capacity for symbolic thought each of us possesses by nature. The realized and consciously understood dream/associational network is both a brilliant work of art and an enormous adaptive resource.

MOSS IS A man in his early forties, a psychologist and psychotherapist. One morning, he woke up and remembered a dream that *his brother Lucas has a metal leg in the form of a rod with a large loop at the upper end, through which the metal limb is attached to his lower body. Lucas is walking with a limp, which Moss actually feels as his own in the dream. Someone has proposed that if Lucas's other leg is broken, and the metal one removed, both can be replaced with normal legs, and Lucas will be able to walk without defect for the rest of his life. The risk seems enormous, and the proposal seems insane, but Lucas decides to go along with the idea.*

At the time of this dream, Moss was a family therapist by profession. He was practicing what is called the systems theory of family therapy, which holds that the family unit functions like other systems found in nature—an aggregation of elements that are mutually interactive and together create a pattern. Moss had recently come to believe that the family system could become so stabilized in a pathological pattern of relationships that only violent destabilization could result in change. In practice, this meant that the therapist was obliged, at times, to treat a family with assault and violence to throw the pathological system into disequilibrium. Moss's experience had been that the resulting chaotic state would generate a new, healthier family system.

In advocating destabilizing interventions, Moss had drawn the criticism of his peers and mentors. He had been threatened with dismissal from a clinic where he worked. On the day of the dream, he had received a letter that questioned his theory and practice from a colleague whose support he had deeply cherished.

Moss assumed immediately that the trigger situation for this dream was his experience with his colleagues—

the fact that his professional integrity was being questioned. With this in mind, he examined the themes from
his manifest dream. In one sense, Moss thought, the reaction of his colleagues was affecting his own self-image;
he was seeing himself as damaged, and crippled. This dream
image had a number of facets, however; the idea of losing
a leg and replacing it with something inadequate and artificial seemed to be a reaction to one solution to his problem. If he gave up his ideas to restore his professional
"standing" in the community, he would be doing so by
artificial means, and he would be crippling his own instincts. The dream seemed to be pointing him in the direction of the more alarming alternative—to risk everything,
even his position in the community, for the sake of feeling
whole and intact, "standing on his own two feet." Clearly,
the dream images were indicating that he should do what
needed to be done, despite the possibility of losing his
standing altogether. The vision of wholeness was more
important than an artificial temporary solution to an immediate problem with his colleagues.

Moss continued to associate to this dream, even though
it had already given him a resourceful direction for the
future of his clinical work. He thought of how his brother
Lucas had been emotionally ill recently, suffering greatly
after the sudden death of one of his children. Bereft with
grief, Lucas's mind had become disorganized and he had
temporarily become psychotic. With the help of intensive
therapy, he was now on the road to recovery. It was as if
a terrible cloud had been lifted, and he was functioning
again at a very high level as a research biologist. Suddenly,
Moss understood another trigger for his dream; he had received a positive and emotionally uplifting telephone call
from his brother on the evening prior to the dream. Emo-

tional illness, and even psychotic symptoms, are a form of disequilibrium, a form of chaos. And yet, Moss thought, sometimes someone who is struggling and unable to cope must move toward greater disequilibrium and chaos before emerging into a new and ultimately steady state—a state of higher and far more adequate functioning.

For Moss, the view of emotional difficulty as a kind of system disequilibrium was a fresh and original insight. The realization pointed him toward further new ideas and helped him to integrate some puzzling clinical observations. And it gave Moss added faith that his work was moving in a productive direction. By trigger-decoding his dream, he now understood something about the psyche that had both personal and general import. On the personal side, Moss now knew that he would have to tolerate professional and personal chaos to emerge at a higher level of integration himself.

As Moss began to rest easy with these insights, he realized that there was another personal message in this dream/associational network. Moss's two-year relationship with his girlfriend, Adele, was going badly. Here was another dysfunctional system, which seemed to be in a permanent state of disequilibrium. He had never thought about it in those terms before, but the relationship was clearly chaotic, with no sign of integration at a higher level. Adele had also called on the night prior to the dream, and there had been the usual arguments. Moss had long been aware that he did not want to break up with Adele because of the depression and lack of stability he typically felt after ending a relationship. And yet the dream/associational network suggested now that if he stayed with Adele, he would feel damaged and crippled for the rest of his life. There was something real and good in the relationship, but its standing depended on something artificial and unhealthy; the dream was suggesting that he sever what was good in the relationship to achieve wholeness in some other way. In terms of the dream image, he had to break it off and to accept the anxiety and disequilibrium out of which something far better might well emerge. Here, too, Moss knew the direction he must now take. Although far from evident on the surface, his dream, by way of trigger decoding, was a reflection and source of great unconscious wisdom and strength.

Moss's deep unconscious intelligence went even further—"it" selected a new woman he might go out with, a woman Moss had not considered at all on the conscious level as a potential romantic interest. From time to time he had talked with an attractive biologist, Melinda, who, now that Moss thought about it, sometimes wore an icon with an ankhlike configuration that much resembled the looped metal limb in his dream. Melinda was bright and warm, and there had been a kind of subtle chemistry between them when they had talked about this and that— mostly topics of great interest to Moss that seemed to interest Melinda as well. It was suddenly clear to Moss that he had been unconsciously working over his problems with Adele for quite some time, and that he was already envisioning his future without her. He hadn't realized that he was prepared to take that risk. He also recognized the kinship between his professional and personal situations: In each arena he had felt damaged and false, but he was holding on to what he had rather than risking the dangers and fears attendant on self-transformation. He remembered now that the ankh was a symbol of life and generation, and felt again that the direction he seemed to be taking in all quarters was sound and whole.

DREAMS, then, serve to help us heal past wounds. They are also forward-looking and point us toward what we may best become. We can only marvel at the ingenuity of the deep unconscious system that powers dream activity. At best, only a few of us are geniuses in our waking, everyday lives. But all of us have a genius inside—an extraordinary deep unconscious system that has been built up over millennia of evolution with enormous and remarkable capacities. And although the system is by no means perfect—when under assault it will often pretend that all is well and deny the danger—it is reassuring to know we have a piece of brilliance within us, ready to be called out and given its due on this side of sleep.

INDEX

About the Author

Robert Langs, M.D. is a visiting clinical investigator at the Nathan S. Kline Institute for Psychiatric Research in Orangeburg, New York, and Clinical Professor of Psychiatry at the Mt. Sinai School of Medicine in New York City. He lectures widely in the U.S. and Europe and is the author of twenty books on psychotherapy including *Madness and Cure* and *Rating Your Psychotherapist*.